Wee Johnny

Stories for Children

by

Harry Pinkerton

Duncerithern Publishing
111, Mussenden Road, Castlerock, BT51 4TU,
Co. Londonderry, N. Ireland
Telephone: (01265) 848276

ISBN 0 9513922 1 2

Illustrations by Steven Brown,
31 Grange Road, Coleraine.
Telephone: (01265) 57906

Printed by Coleraine Printing Company,
117 Ballycastle Road, Coleraine, BT52 2DZ.
Telephone: (01265) 54873 / 58412

Wee Johnny

Stories for Children

Foreword

by
The Very Rev. William Boyd,
M.A., D.D.

I have accepted gladly Mrs. Mary Pinkerton's suggestion to write a brief foreword, introducing these "Wee Johnny" children's addresses which were preached by her husband during his ministry.

I knew the Rev. R.H. Pinkerton from his student days at Magee. His home church was The Mall, Armagh and during my ministry there I got to know his parents and family and so I appreciate that Harry's love for the church and his dedication to its work originated in his home.

He had a very definite calling to the ministry of the church and he always maintained that the church - not only its ministers but its people - must recognise their calling. We all are to be in the world as a sign and a light, and the splendour of the church depends upon all who are its members. Foremost among its membership, in his mind, were the children and young people and these children's addresses which began in Muckamore, where he was ordained, continued right through his ministry in Trinity, Omagh and Gillygooley and finally in Edenderry.

What a delight it will be to all these people, and many others beside, to be able to see in print these talks which brought such a challenge to so many.

I commend it warmly and wish it the success it deserves.

Preface

"Wee Johnny" was born in 1939 in my husband's first congregation in Muckamore, Co. Antrim. The Church was in the townland of Shanoguestown which means "the town of little John" and so "Wee Johnny" came into being. He later moved with us to Omagh in 1943 and finally to Edenderry in 1970.

"Wee Johnny" was a little imaginary friend of the boys and girls, a Peter Pan character whose exploits the children (and older folk as well) looked forward to hearing about each Sunday.

Over a period of forty-five years "Wee Johnny" became a very real character to the boys and girls who knew him and loved him.

This book is a collection of some of the many "Wee Johnny" stories told by my husband over the years. Harry loved young people, he had a wonderful way of making friends with them and with his natural gift for story telling these "Wee Johnny" stories came alive.

I am pleased that I have been able to recreate "Wee Johnny" and I hope that these stories will bring much pleasure to many people.

I would like to thank most sincerely a good friend of "Wee Johnny's" for the financial support which has made the publication of this book possible. I also owe a great debt of gratitude to the Rev. John McCaughan for encouraging me to publish these stories and introducing me to his son and daughter-in-law, the Rev. Jim & Alison McCaughan who have edited this book and made arrangements for its printing.

Mary Pinkerton
81, Edenderry Road,
Omagh

In memory of Harry

What Wee Johnny meant to me

by
The Rev. Charles J.C. McMullen,
M.A. M. Litt, B.D.

For this child of the 1960s there was always eager anticipation on a Sunday morning. It was such a disappointment when, for whatever reason, there was no "Wee Johnny" story. Indeed so uncharitable was I that I dreaded a visiting minister who, for some mysterious reason, had never heard of "Wee Johnny"! The first two hymns, the prayer and the reading seemed long as I waited to discover what my friend had been doing during the course of the week. Then came those marvellous words: "Boys and Girls . . . "

Wee Johnny was my friend. I could identify with him. He had the same thoughts and ideas about life. He had the same loving parents and went to the same kind of school. It was good that he was never above doing wrong which meant that I could learn from his mistakes. Above all, he loved Jesus and taught me to do likewise.

Once the children's hymn was sung, we trooped out to Sunday School which was held in the "Wee Johnny Room". This place was a focal point and with its name association helped us to relax, to feel at home and to learn about the faith. It was the children of the Sunday School who in 1957 formed the "Wee Johnny Club" which raised money in order to furnish this room, and we enjoyed the benefits of their work.

For me it is a privilege now to introduce "Wee Johnny" to a wider audience, and an opportunity to indulge in nostalgia. In retrospect, the Rev. Harry Pinkerton told these stories with simple, homely, endearing charm, and his own childlike faith made a real impression on me. How he sustained "Wee Johnny" over the years I shall never know, but I thank God for his ministry to children - both young and old - in Trinity Presbyterian Church, Omagh.

About the author

Robert Harold Pinkerton was born in Armagh in 1913. He attended the Royal School, Armagh and later Magee University College, Trinity College, Dublin (where he graduated in 1935) and finally Assembly's College, Belfast from 1935 - 1937.

He was then assistant minister in Cooke Centenary Church, Belfast and was ordained to his first charge in Muckamore Presbyterian Church in 1939. In 1943, he moved to Trinity and Gillygooley Presbyterian Churches in the Omagh Presbytery, and in 1970 became minister of Edenderry Presbyterian Church from which he retired in 1979.

The Rev. R.H. Pinkerton died in 1985.

How "Wee Johnny" came about

Boys and girls have you ever wondered about 'Wee Johnny' - where he was born or how he came into existence? Let me tell you.

Over 40 years ago when I was ordained in my first church, Muckamore Presbyterian Church - near Antrim town, the Church was in the townland of "Shanoguestown" and this is where Wee Johnny was born.

He got his name from Shanoguestown because "Shan" means "John" in Irish and "Ogue" is the Irish for "Little" or "Small".

So you see the whole word means Little Johnstown. Little John became Wee Johnny and I have been telling boys and girls about him ever since.

Johnny takes up the offering

One Sunday there was a special service for children in the Church and the offering was to be taken by the boys and girls. Johnny was to do the first four pews on the left hand side. When they had finished they were to go to the back and all walk up together. What do you think happened? All the people crushed into the back part of the church and there wasn't a single person sitting in the seats where Johnny had to collect. One of the other boys who was to collect whispered to Johnny "You needn't get up at all".

But Johnny wasn't going to be as easily put off as that. When the offering was announced, he got up with others. He walked up to the front and got his offering plate and then, very slowly, he walked past all the empty seats right down to the back of the church. There he waited for the other collectors. When they had finished he walked up with the others and put his plate on the table at the front and then walked back with them to his own pew.

When they got home his Daddy said, "Man, Johnny, you're a silly boy. Why did you get up at all when there was nobody in your seats?". "Why not?" asked Johnny. "Why not?" repeated his Daddy, "Because you hadn't anything on your plate". "Oh yes, I had", said Johnny, "I had my own offering".

Johnny was right. For his offering, although it didn't amount to much was just as important as any of the others.

Jesus taught us this lesson when he saw the poor widow coming into the Temple and putting her two mites in the offering. She had the smallest offering, but in God's sight it was the best of all. God doesn't count what amount we give but the sacrifice it means to us, and above all the spirit in which we give.

(Money: the Offering, Mark ch. 12, vs. 41-44)

A game of marbles

One day wee Johnny brought a little friend home with him after school. Both of them had their pockets full of marbles and so they decided to have a game. They drew a circle on the ground and in it they both put 6 of the little marbles. They drew a straight line to mark the start. Each boy played in turn and whatever marbles they managed to knock out of the circle they kept for themselves. But Johnny wasn't playing well and no matter how hard he tried he just couldn't shoot straight. His little friend was knocking the marbles out of the circle and putting them in his pocket. And Johnny wasn't too pleased. It wasn't long before Johnny lost all his marbles, but he lost more than his marbles, he lost his temper. He threw his big glassy marbles into the hedge, stamped his feet on the ground and, almost in tears, ran into the house without even saying good-bye to his friend. His Mammy had been watching and when Johnny came in she didn't say much. She simply told him to wash his hands and start his lessons. But when Johnny's Daddy came home she told him what had happened. He said to Johnny, "Do you know what happens to wee boys who lose their temper at a game and stamp their feet on the ground?" "Yes", said Johnny, " they grow up to play golf". Everybody laughed and the game of marbles was not mentioned again. When Johnny went to bed that night he said his prayers. He asked God to forgive him for losing his temper and to help him always to play the game even if he wasn't winning.

Next morning when he went to school he said sorry to his little friend. So, although Johnny lost his temper and lost his marbles he didn't lose his friend. Johnny had the good sense to see he had made a mistake and had the grace to go and say he was sorry.

(Temper: Matthew ch. 5 vs. 23, 24)

One sided view

Wee Johnny and his friend Jimmy are very interested in military vehicles and they know all the names of the different types of army lorries and armoured cars.

One day, they were out walking along a country road and they weren't thinking much about where they were walking, when suddenly there was the sound of a lorry and the blowing of a horn. Johnny jumped to one side of the road and Jimmy to the other and a big military lorry swished in between them. "Boys", said Johnny, "that was going at some speed". Then the two boys started to talk about the lorry. Johnny said that it was brown and Jimmy argued that it was grey. Johnny said, "I know it was brown, I'm sure of it". Jimmy said, "I know it was grey, I'm sure of it". They continued to argue and walked on and soon they discovered the lorry had stopped further down the road.

They both began to run and Johnny said, "Now we'll soon see who's right". When they got up to the lorry, they found that it was camouflaged and that one side was brown and the other side was grey. So, in a way, they were both right and they were both wrong because they had seen the lorry from different sides.

Boys and girls and grown ups, too, are often like that. They don't try to see each other's point of view. Sometimes they start stupid and silly quarrels when all the time the other person is just as right as they are. They just see it from a different side. Always try to see both sides and remember other people are entitled to their own opinions.

(Arguments: 2 Timothy ch. 2 v. 23, Titus ch. 3 v. 9)

The hole in the hedge

One day wee Johnny brought some of his school friends home after school to play with him. It was a good day and they were playing outside. There was a lot of traffic on the road and they were running in and out of the gate.

Every now and then his Mammy could hear the cars hooting their horns as they passed. She went outside and closed the gate and said to them all, "Now don't go out of the gate again". And she went back into the house. Before long she heard the cars hooting again and, when she looked out, Johnny and his friends were out on the road. She rushed out. "I thought I told you not to go out of the gate", she said. She was very angry., "We didn't go out of the gate", answered Johnny, "we went out through the hole in the hedge".

Now I suppose you could say Johnny hadn't been disobedient. He hadn't gone out of the gate but he knew in his own heart he had done wrong. He had kept the letter of the law but he had broken the spirit of the law. And we are tempted to do that in life. In the Old Testament God laid down certain laws for His children - The Ten Commandments. But true faith goes far beyond the keeping of the law. In the teaching of Jesus we learn that what counts is not so much the strict observance of the letter of the law, as the spirit of obedience in the heart of His children. Remember that and give yourself gladly to the service of God.

(Law: 2 Corinthians ch. 3 v. 6)

Why should we save our pennies

One Sunday, in Johnny's class in Sunday School, there was a missionary lesson. The teacher told the boys and girls about Africa, to show why we should send missionaries and money. She explained that in some parts of Africa the boys and girls didn't go to church because there was no church. They didn't go to school to learn to read and write and do arithmetic because there were no schools.

"Now why do you think", said the teacher, "that we should all save our pennies?" "Please Miss", said wee Johnny, "to get the money to go to Africa". You see Johnny thought it would be great not to have to go to school or do lessons. But of course he was wrong because we go to school to learn things to help us in life. That is why in our missionary work we not only build churches, but we also build schools and hospitals. That is why we send out not only preachers but also teachers, doctors and nurses.

It is in obedience to Jesus' command that our missionaries go to tell others of His love. For the same reason we give our money that boys and girls all over the world may learn about Jesus and come to share the many blessings which we all enjoy.

(Giving/ Missionaries: Matthew ch. 28 v. 19; 2 Corinthians ch. 8 vs. 1-4)

Magic match box

During the summer holidays wee Johnny spent part of the time staying with his cousins in the country. He was staying there because his Mammy and Daddy had gone for a short holiday to France.

When they were there, they bought some things to take home. Johnny's Daddy bought him a magic match box. The shop assistant said it would glow brightly in the dark.

The first night they were at home his Daddy thought he would give Johnny a surprise. He asked him to turn off all the lights and then he slipped the magic match box on to his knee. But he got a 'gunk' - for it was just as dark as the darkness all around. He thought he had been "done" and he was disappointed. When Johnny was going to bed he took the box with him and he saw the instructions painted on the back of it. They were written in French so Johnny took it to school and asked the French teacher what it meant.

A few nights later Johnny switched out the lights and he said, "Now look at the magic match box on the mantelpiece". There it was glittering and glowing in the darkness. His Daddy asked him what had he done and he said he had just followed the instructions. These said:-

"If you keep me in the sunshine all day long

I'll shine for you the whole night through".

In just the same way, if you and I want to be bright and cheerful and able to shine in the darkness of the world - we need to know the secret. The secret is to live in the sunshine of God's presence. Then we can be, what Jesus expects us to be - as he said in the sermon on the mount - "You are the light of the world".

(Witness, Light: Matthew ch. 5 vs. 14-16, 2 Corinthians ch. 3 v. 18)

Holidays from Church

On the first Saturday of July wee Johnny was allowed to sit up later than usual. He was allowed to watch a film on television. When it was over it was after ten and his Daddy told him to go to bed. But it was one of those nights when Johnny didn't want to go to bed, and he asked to wait up to see the next programme. "Sure it doesn't matter about being late tonight", he said, "I can lie to dinner time tomorrow. We have our holidays from school, and our holidays from Sunday School and we might as well take a holiday from Church". "Well", said his Daddy, "you can stay up if you like but we'll all be going to Church as usual in the morning". Johnny said to his Daddy, "Why do we get holidays from school and Sunday School but no holidays from Church?" His Daddy said, "You go to school to learn things that will be useful to you and you go to Sunday School to learn about God but that's not why you go to Church. You go to Church because God has made Sunday to be a day of rest and worship. You go to Church to worship God and one of the commandments is 'Remember the Sabbath day to keep it holy'. And after all God never takes a holiday. It would be too bad for us if He did, for every day we need His help. His goodness and mercy follow us all the days of our lives, without a holiday and without a break. His mercy is fresh every morning and is renewed each night".

"I never thought of it like that", said Johnny.

So Johnny went to bed and in the morning when he woke up and remembered that it was Sunday, he said a little prayer. This is what he prayed "This is the day which the Lord has made, we will rejoice and be glad in it".

Then he hopped out of bed and with a happy heart he got ready for Church.

(Sunday: Psalm 118 v. 24)

Make all the bad people good and make all the good people nice

One day wee Johnny asked his Mammy, "Do you think that we should pray for our enemies?" "Well", said his Mammy, "Jesus told us to pray for those who despitefully use you and persecute you and that would mean your enemies". Johnny thought about this but didn't say very much. Next morning he said to his Mammy, "I prayed for my enemies last night. I prayed for everybody in the world. I asked God to make all the bad people good and all the good people nice".

We can learn many lessons from Johnny's prayer. First of all we can learn to follow the example of Jesus and remember in our prayers all kinds of people.

Then we can learn that the world is divided in two, not just east and west. But in the sight of God the world is divided by good and bad. There is no other division in the sight of God. That is why Jesus said, "He that is not for me is against me". Lastly we can learn from the fact that there are some good people who are not always nice.

People who follow Jesus should be happy and glad but sometimes religion makes them glum and cranky. Everyone who follows Jesus should go about the world with a happy heart. If we would all do our best to do that there would be no need for a prayer like this, "O God make all the bad people good and the good people nice".

(Prayer: Luke ch. 6 v. 28 and ch. 11 v. 23)

Johnny's marbles

Boys and girls wee Johnny has had a great time lately playing marbles and he's very good at it. I'm sure you all know how to play. First of all you make a circle on the ground and then the players put two, three or four small marbles into the centre. Then each player takes it in turn to play his own marble to try to knock the small marbles out of the circle. Of course any you knock out you keep. Well on Saturday wee Johnny was playing very well and at the end of the afternoon he had won so many marbles that his trouser pockets were bulging. It was a very happy little boy who went to bed that night. On Sunday morning when he came down to breakfast, dressed and ready for Church, his Mammy said to him, "What have you got in your pockets Johnny?" "Marbles", said Johnny. "Well", said his Mammy, "if you take my advice you'll go upstairs and leave them in your bedroom". "But I want to show them to the boys in Sunday School", said Johnny. So he set off with his pockets full of marbles.

When he was in Church, in the middle of a prayer, when all was quiet, Johnny felt as if he was going to sneeze. He pulled out his handkerchief and along with it, a pocket full of marbles. With a terrible clatter they fell onto the seat and then one by one they dropped onto the floor. Poor Johnny!! Everyone was looking at him. He never felt so ashamed of himself in his life. So Johnny went home a very thoughtful and a very humble boy. On that day he learned two lessons which he never forgot.

The first was, that in future, he would listen to his mother's advice. The second was, that never again would he do anything in Church that would disturb the service or annoy the people of the congregation. It would be a good thing if all the boys and girls, both young and old, would make the same resolve that Johnny made.

(Worship)

The Queen's visit

Did I ever tell you that wee Johnny saw the Queen and the Duke of Edinburgh when they visited Northern Ireland? His Mammy took him and they got a good place very near to where the Queen was passing. Johnny was very impressed with the Queen. He was so much impressed that he was silent for a long time, evidently deep in thought.

At last his Mammy managed to coax him to tell her what he was thinking. "I was thinking", he said, "how lucky Prince Charles is to have such a lovely Mammy".

But you know boys and girls, Prince Charles isn't the only fortunate child, for we should all be thankful that we, too, have lovely Mammies. Not one of you, I am sure, would want to change, even for a Queen. You wouldn't change your Mammy for all the money in the world. And I tell you why - because you owe more to your mother than you will ever be able to repay. We should all try to show that we appreciate how much we owe to our parents. There are lots of ways every boy and girl can do that. You can do it at home by being kind, obedient, considerate and helpful. I hope you will begin to do this today (Mother's Day). Every day you fail to do this simple duty is a day of lost opportunity and believe me if you lose this opportunity the time will surely come when you will be filled with sorrow and regret.

(Mother's Day)

Imposing on kindness

One day wee Johnny had a school friend in to play with him and when they were playing, who should call but Johnny's Uncle Bill. He spoke to the boys and then he put his hand into his trouser pocket and took out all his money. He held it out on his hand before Johnny. He must have done it often before, because immediately Johnny began to pick out all the 1p and 2p pieces and put them in his own pocket. Johnny's friend kept watching it with big open eyes and wished he had an Uncle Bill like that.

When the two boys were alone Johnny explained that every time his uncle called he held out his money in his hand and Johnny picked out all the copper coins and kept them for himself. "He didn't tell you to take the coppers", said his friend. "You're silly not to take the silver". "Indeed I'm not", said Johnny, "for if I took the silver once, I'm sure he would never offer it to me again".

Johnny had learned a very wise lesson. If you impose on kindness when it is offered, it is not likely to be offered to you again.

A shopkeeper held out a jar of sweets to a little boy to help himself. He put in his hand and filled his fist as full of sweets as he could but he found he had made a mistake because he had to open his hand to get it out of the bottle and he lost everything.

Boys and girls, it is never a good thing to impose on kindness. Learn when people are good to you not to be greedy. Try to repay a little for all the kindness which others show to you and also pass the kindness on to someone else.

(Greed)

Different languages

When wee Johnny began to learn languages at school he was doing French and German. When he had learned a few words he came home from school one day and announced that he could talk three languages - English, French and German. "There's something else you can sometimes talk too", said his Mammy, "you can talk back". To talk back isn't a very nice thing for any boy or girl to do, no matter how many languages you learn. I hope you will not "talk back", especially to your mother.

When we were in Wales on holiday, on Sunday we went to church and the service was in Welsh. I read once about a Welsh girl who went to work in England. She found a church where the service was in Welsh but it was a long way from where she stayed. But every Sunday she walked the long distance to worship in her own language. Her friends invited her to go with them to their church. "You know", they said, "Jesus wasn't a Welshman". "I know that", said the girl, "but it's in Welsh he speaks to me". Isn't it wonderful that all the millions of people in the world can speak to God in thousands of different languages and he can understand them all in their own tongue. God knows all the people of the world and loves them each one.

'Jesus loves the Indian boy, bow and arrow for his toy,

Big Philippino, wee Chinese, living far across the seas,

Jesus loves the Eskimo from the land of ice and snow,

And he loves the cowboy too with his horse and rope lasso'.

"God loves us all as if there were but one of us to love".

(Worldwide Mission)

Race course - Two laps

In the class at school wee Johnny was doing problems about averages and he was fairly good at them. So was his friend Jimmy. On the way home from school Johnny said, "Those maths problems are too easy". "Well", said Jimmy, "I'll give you one that's not so simple. It's about a race course and a motor car. The race course was a circle and it was exactly 1 mile around it. The driver had to do two laps and he had to average a speed of 60 m.p.h. On the first lap he had a mechanical fault and he could only average 30 m.p.h. This was the problem - at what speed would he need to do the second lap to average 60 m.p.h. for the two laps?"

Johnny thought for a minute and then he said "90". "No", said Jimmy. Johnny thought again and decided it must be 90, for 30 and 90 are 120 and 120 divided by 2 is 60.

"That's not the right answer". said Jimmy, "Ask your Daddy that one". So Johnny asked his Daddy and his Daddy thought a moment and then said "It can't be done. The driver had to do 2 laps, that is 2 miles at 60 m.p.h. or a mile a minute so 2 miles would take 2 minutes. But when he had done the first lap at 30 m.p.h., he took 2 minutes so he had already used up all his time and no matter how hard he tried he could never average 60 m.p.h for the 2 laps".

It's a good puzzle and it teaches us a good lesson. That we should never put off to tomorrow what we can do today. Often we get the chance of being kind to somebody, or helping somebody or doing something unselfish, but if we don't do it at the time we may never have another chance. This is true of many things in life, but it is especially true of serving and following Jesus. That is why it tells us in the Bible - "Now is the accepted time, now is the day of salvation".

(Opportunity: 2 Cor. ch. 6, v. 2)

Rent free

One time wee Johnny thought that he would like to keep a few hens. His Mammy said it would be all right if he did all the work with them. She bought him six young hens that were just starting to lay and they made a little run for them at the bottom of the garden.

Soon Johnny started to get some eggs. Some days two, sometimes three or four or even six. Johnny looked after them very well. One day a visitor said to Johnny, "What do you do with the eggs?" "Well", said Johnny, "I sell them to Mammy for 10p each". "You don't get enough for them, you should get 12p at least", said the visitor. "Oh I know that", said Johnny, "but then you see I get the run rent free".

It's a good thing to see that Johnny had some thought for the things he got for nothing.

Sometimes boys and girls, we are tempted to forget things like that. When we think of all that is given to us freely, surely the least we can do is to be grateful. We get our food, our clothes, our books, our games, our toys and a host of other things all given to us. And what do they cost us - nothing. They are given to us freely, without charge. Never forget, boys and girls, how much you owe to those who love you and always try to show your thankfulness.

(Gratitude)

God forgives and forgets

One day wee Johnny did something that was very naughty indeed. He felt very ashamed of himself and he was truly sorry that he had done it. He was so ashamed of it that he didn't want anybody to know about it.

Every night when wee Johnny went to bed his Mammy always came in to tuck him up and to say good-night. She always read to him and then they said a prayer together.

This night when his Mammy came to say good-night Johnny said, "I want to say my prayers by myself tonight". "That's all right", said his Mammy, "but is there something you can't tell me?" "Well I could tell you", said Johnny, "but if I did, I know you would scold me. But when I tell God and ask for His forgiveness - He just forgives and forgets".

Isn't it wonderful to have a God like that who forgives and forgets. This is the God that Jesus came to show us. Let us open our hearts to Him. Even when we have done wrong, if we confess and forsake our sin, He is willing and ready to forgive.

*(Repentance:
1 John ch. 1 v. 9)*

The Big Gun from Belfast

One Sunday night, not long ago, wee Johnny was allowed to stay up late to go to a Harvest Service in a church in the country.

The church was decorated with flowers, fruit and vegetables. The choir sang an anthem and there was a soloist and of course a special preacher from Belfast. After church they invited some people home for supper and there was a lot of chat about the service. When wee Johnny went to bed he started to think about all the remarks he had heard about the service and in his own imagination he drew a very funny picture.

Next day at school he was telling one of his friends about the service. "There was a terrible row at church last night you know", said Johnny. "To begin with", said Johnny, "the organist drowned the soloist and then the choir murdered the anthem and to crown it all they had a big gun from Belfast in the pulpit". Of course Johnny was only joking because he knew perfectly well what was meant by the remarks but it goes to show how a simple saying can be twisted to mean something that was never intended.

Boys and girls, we should always be careful of what we say about others and if, by any chance, you hear somebody talking about somebody else and it's not a nice thing, then keep it to yourself. God has given us all the wonderful power of speech, a mind to reason, with a heart to love with. We should always try to let our thoughts and words be guided by a heart of love.

(Speech: Psalm 141, v. 3)

Good for nothing

One day wee Johnny's Mammy was having some special visitors to tea. For two or three days she had been busy in the house, baking and tidying. Of course everybody in the house had to do something to help. But Johnny's Mammy had one big worry and that was Johnny. She was always a bit nervous when there were visitors, for she never knew what Johnny would do or what he would say. But on this particular occasion he was well warned. "When you come home from school", said his Mammy, "the visitors will be here, so don't go dashing about the house. Come in and say 'hello' and then go and start your lessons. Make sure your hands and face are clean". "It's not going to be much of a party", said Johnny. "Maybe not", said his Mammy, "but promise me, please, for once you'll be good". Then Johnny's face lit up with a mischievous smile. "What will you give me if I'm good?" he asked. "Johnny dear, are you never going to grow up!" said his Mammy, "Such a thing for a boy of your age to ask - what will I give you if you are good? Why can't you be like your Daddy and be good for nothing!"

You know when Johnny asked, "What will you give me if I'm good?" he was following the example of the disciples. They came to Jesus and asked him what they would get for following him. And Jesus gave them a wonderful promise. He told them they would get one hundred fold now, and in the world to come, eternal life. So you see goodness is always rewarded, especially the goodness of those who love Jesus and are ready to follow him.

(Rewards: Matthew ch. 19, vs. 27-29)

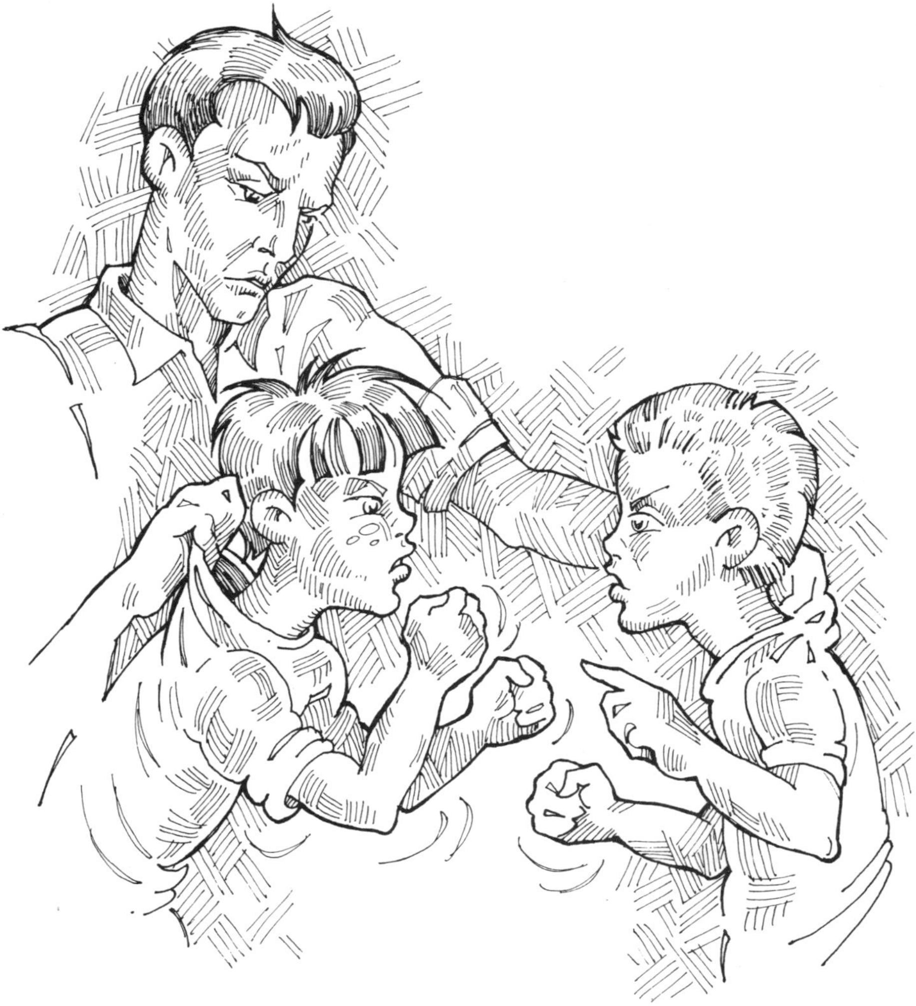

Johnny's repentance

One Saturday wee Johnny invited one of his school friends out to his house for the afternoon. But before the afternoon was over, they fell out and began to fight. They weren't right started when Johnny's Daddy appeared, so he separated them and told Johnny to apologise. "I'm sorry for hitting you", said Johnny. "You're not a bit sorry", said his friend.

"I am sorry", said Johnny. "You're not", said his friend. Then Johnny turned to his Daddy - "Amn't I sorry?" he asked. "Of course you are Johnny", said his Daddy.

"There now", said Johnny as if that was the end of it. "Daddy said I'm sorry". "You are not sorry" - "I am" - "You're not".

Johnny could stand it no longer - he just closed his fist and hit his friend a crack on the face and shouted, "Don't you dare say I'm not sorry when I say I am".

Poor Johnny! He didn't really know what he was doing or what he was saying. But down at the bottom of his heart he wasn't really sorry at all.

For when you do something wrong and are really sorry for it, you always try your best not to do it again.

This is what it means in the Bible when it tells us to confess and forsake our sin. That is what we call true repentance - or true sorrow, not just saying "I'm sorry", but trying at the same time not to fall into the same sin again.

(Repentance)

Getting in free

Johnny had a friend at school called Tom and Tom didn't go to Church or Sunday School. Johnny asked Tom to come to Church with him and he said he would call for him on Sunday morning. Tom told his parents he was going to Church on Sunday with his friend Johnny.

Tom's Mammy looked out some clean clothes for him to wear and gave him 10p for the offering. Tom went to Church and arrived home eating sweets. "Where did you get the sweets Tom?" asked his Mammy. "I bought them with the 10p", said Tom, "because I hadn't to pay to get in". Of course nobody pays to get into Church although people who belong to the Church usually pay to support it.

But there is another place, even more important than Church, that nobody has to pay to get into and that is heaven. I heard an old song on the radio recently. One of the verses went like this:

"You'll never get to heaven with a bar of gold, for up there things aren't bought or sold".

Nobody has to pay to get into heaven because Jesus, by His life, His death and His resurrection has already paid the price and opened the way for all who follow Him to get into heaven free. You'll never get to heaven with a bar of gold. The only way is by loving, serving and following Jesus.

(Heaven: John ch. 14 v. 6)

Potatoes

Johnny was in the garden watching his Daddy at work. He was sowing potatoes. He saw him take the potatoes and bury them in the ground. "What a waste of good potatoes", said Johnny, "Why do you bury them like that?"

His Daddy told him to wait and see. The weeks and months passed and Johnny didn't forget the potatoes. Every now and then he would ask about them and his Daddy kept saying, "Oh, just you wait and see". One day Johnny was so impatient he slipped down to the garden and dug up one of the potatoes to find, as he expected, a rotten potato. "I knew it", he said, "just a waste of a good potato". He told his Daddy what he had done but his Daddy just said, "Wait and see".

Then one day during the school holidays his Daddy called him and said, "Come with me Johnny. We are going to do some digging". And so to Johnny's amazement the potato that he thought was lost had produced a whole crop of new ones.

You see Johnny had forgotten that God was working. That's what happened when Jesus was dead and buried. They thought he was lost and gone for ever but they had forgotten that God was working. For Jesus came back and now he is alive for evermore. What a wonderful day Easter Sunday is!

(Easter:
Romans ch. 6 v. 4)

God so loved the world

Boys and girls I wonder if any of you ever feel not too well in the morning, especially when you haven't got your lessons done. You have a headache, you can't eat your breakfast but it's wonderful how quickly you get better if you are allowed to stay at home. I used to be like that when I was young. But one morning I was really ill. When the doctor came he said I had appendicitis and before long, I was in hospital and had my appendix out. I was just ten and I can remember how I spent the time in hospital. I read lots of comics and then my mother taught me to knit. I know you think that's a cissy kind of a thing for a boy, but I knitted myself a pair of football socks and many times I wore them playing rugby at school. Then I remember my mother used to read to me and I will never forget one verse from the Bible which she read and which influenced my whole life. It was John 3:16 "For God so loved the world that He gave His only begotten Son that whosoever believeth in Him should not perish but have everlasting life".

It was through this verse that I first realised the wonder of God's love and the wonder of Jesus' love in giving His life on the cross. It was then I realised that God loved all the world and that He loved me so much that He was ready to die for my sin. And when I thought of that, I offered myself to God's service and I never had any other purpose in life but to be a minister. I rejoice today that I was brought into the kingdom and that I was, through the years, strengthened and encouraged in my faith by the influence and example of my mother's love. I would like to pass on to you the message of this text. "For God so loved the world that He gave His only begotten Son that whosoever believeth in Him should not perish but have everlasting life".

There is nothing would bring greater joy to my heart than that you boys and girls should respond to God's love as I did in my early days - by giving your life in service to Christ. There is no greater thing that anyone can do.

(This address was given to the children on the Sunday after the death of Mr. Pinkerton's mother).

(Giving your life to Jesus: John ch. 3 v. 16)

Johnny's sums - perfect

When wee Johnny started to do sums at school his teacher told him to practise them at home and for a couple of weeks he kept everyone busy. Whenever he saw anyone at home with nothing to do he would say, "Give me some sums please?"

One day his Mammy was at home by herself, and she thought she would give him really hard ones and this would keep him busy for some time. Johnny settled down at the table and he spent a long time working them all out. At last he was finished and he asked his Mammy to mark them. So she got a red pencil and ticked each sum that was correct and what do you think? He got them all right. She gave Johnny a pat on the back and said, "That's very good Johnny". "What do you mean, 'very good'?" Johnny answered, "Sure, it's perfect". And of course it was. There couldn't be anything more perfect, because they were all correct.

You see Johnny had set himself a high standard - nothing less than perfection. That's a very good thing to do - not just in your sums but in everything - perfection. To-day is the first Sunday of the New Year and what better could we do than set that before us and make it our aim. It will mean we will come every Sunday to Church and Sunday School. That we will always do our lessons well both for Sunday School and Day School. It will mean that we always be kind, gentle, generous and true - it will mean, in a word, that we will be like Jesus. Although this is a very high standard, it is what Jesus asks us to do - "Be ye therefore perfect, even as your Father which is in heaven is perfect". Will you try to do that this year? If you fail or make a mistake don't be discouraged but ask for God's forgiveness and start all over again.

(New Year: Matthew ch. 5 v. 48)

The fairy and the false tooth

There was always great excitement in wee Johnny's house when Johnny lost a tooth. He got a tumbler of water and hid it away in a quiet place with the little tooth in it. Then the fairies came when nobody was about. They took the tooth away and left some money in the glass to pay for it. One day Johnny's sister fell and broke one of her front teeth. It was one of her second teeth and it would never grow again. She had to go to the dentist and she got a new tooth on a tiny plate which she can take out and put in again. The first night her Mammy told her to take out her tooth and put it in a glass of water beside her bed. When Johnny got into bed, he started to think about his sister's tooth. Then he suddenly jumped out of bed and rushed down to his Mammy. "If Mary leaves her tooth in a glass, the fairies will take it", shouted Johnny. "Don't worry about the fairies", said his Mammy, "they are not easily deceived. They know the difference between a real tooth and a false one and they won't touch it".

Surely there is a lesson in that for us. You know sometimes people make us believe they are different from what they really are. We have a name for people like that - we call them hypocrites. Although they may sometimes deceive people, they can never deceive God.

God sees through all our shams and He knows the difference between the true and the false. We should always try to do what is right in the sight of God for He can never be deceived.

(Hypocrites: Matthew ch. 23 vs. 27-29)

Betty's Party

I want to tell you about a piece of poetry I learned at school a long time ago. It is called Betty's Party and this is how it goes.

"When I was at a party", said Betty, aged just four,
"A little girl fell off her chair, right down upon the floor
And all the other boys and girls began to laugh - but me
I didn't laugh a single bit", said Betty seriously
"Why not?" her mother asked me - full of joy to find
That Betty, bless her little heart, had been so sweetly kind.
"Why didn't you laugh, my darling, or don't you want to tell?"
"I didn't laugh", said Betty, "because it was I, who fell".

You know there are people who are actually pleased when somebody else makes a mistake and they are not very happy when they go wrong themselves. Instead of that we should always be sorry for anyone in trouble and never laugh at the mistakes of others.

Do you remember what Paul wrote about this - "Love rejoiceth not in iniquity" - or love is never glad when others go wrong. How many remember the Golden Rule. It is "Do unto others as you would like them to do unto you".

(The Golden Rule: 1 Corinthians ch. 13 v. 6)

Three lazy sons

The story today is about a farmer who had three lazy sons. One day he told them that he was going away. He said he was going to give each of them a field and in each field there was hidden treasure and when they found it they would be very much richer. Then the farmer went away for a long holiday and left the sons to get on with it. There were no tractors or ploughs in those days and so they had to dig with spades.

When they didn't find any hidden treasure they began to dig deeper and deeper all over the fields. Still they did not find any treasure and, of course, they were disappointed and annoyed. They sowed the fields with seed and when it came to harvest time, to their surprise they had a magnificent crop, the best they had ever seen. They were able to gather three times more than ever before.

At the end of the harvest the father came home and asked his sons how they had got on. Grumbling and complaining they told him they had found no hidden treasure as he had promised. "But what kind of crops did you have?"he asked. "We had the best harvest we ever had", they replied.

Then the father explained that was the hidden treasure - the good harvest. By digging deep and doing it thoroughly they had reaped a wonderful harvest. In this way they learned the value of hard work, well done. That is a lesson all of us need to learn. God gives us all certain talents and a limited number of opportunities. But if we are lazy and let those opportunities slip, or do not use our talents we will never make much of our lives. I knew a home where there was a motto painted over the fire place "Hard work is the road to success and there is no other". I hope that you boys and girls will remember that and whatever gifts God has given you, let them not be wasted in idleness but use them to the full in the service of God.

(Harvest, Laziness: Galatians ch. 6 vs. 7-10, 2 Timothy ch. 2 v. 6)

Johnny's homework

All last week wee Johnny's Daddy and Mammy were away from home and Johnny was left with a lady who had come to keep house and look after him. She was to get him ready for school, make his breakfast and when he came home from school she was to make his tea and get him to bed in good time. Johnny was quite excited because it was the first time his Mammy had left him and he felt quite grown up.

The only thing was that, every night, Johnny needed help and encouragement with his homework. What was he going to do? "Don't worry", said his Mammy, "I'll write a note to your teacher and everything will be all right". So on Monday morning Johnny arrived at school with the note and this is what it said: -

"Please do not give Johnny any problems this week as his Daddy and I will be away and the housekeeper can't do them". What do you think of that? Well I know one thing if Johnny stays at school as long as some boys and girls he'll soon be doing homework that even his Daddy and Mammy won't be able to do! Then he will have to do it for himself.

It is a good thing to remember that there are other things in life as well as homework which we have to do for ourselves. As we get older we discover we have to make our own decisions about many things. The most important thing we have to decide is what we will do with our lives. I don't mean just what occupation we will follow but what we will do with our lives. Will we live simply for our own selfish ends or will we give ourselves to the service of God? That is the most important decision of all and we have to make it for ourselves.

I just want to tell you, no matter what occupation you intend to follow, nothing will bring you greater happiness and peace than living your life to the glory of God in the service of Jesus and His Kingdom in the world.

(Decisions: Joshua ch. 24 v. 15; 1 Kings ch. 18 vs. 21, 39)

Name tapes

Boys and girls I suppose you've all got over the excitement of going back to school. It's great fun going back to school after the long summer holidays. Wee Johnny had been getting new clothes and new books. At school he was in a new class and he had made some new friends. There's always great preparation at the beginning of the term getting everything ready. Johnny's Mammy had been busy getting Johnny's name tapes sewn on to all his clothes and Johnny had written his name on all his belongings. He had his name on all his books, on his pens and pencilcase and even on his ruler. He had his name written all over his school bag, on his sports bag and even on his lunch box. Certainly Johnny was going to make sure if he lost anything it wouldn't be lost forever but could be (he hoped) returned to him.

Sometimes boys and girls, and older people too, wear a name disc around their necks so that if they ever get lost or are in an accident they can be identified. During the Second World War when the children were being sent away from the cities into the country, each child had a label with his name and destination on it.

Once a little dog was being sent by train and it had a label round its neck but at the end of the journey the dog had chewed the label and nobody knew where to send it. In the journey of life there are many places where we might easily get lost, but God has given us many things to guide us. Our parents who love and advise us, schools to teach us, Church and Sunday School to help us. Learn to respect the help of those who are older and wiser and, above all, take Jesus as your guide and He will bring you in safety to the end of the journey.

(Guide: Psalm 48 v. 14)

"Trying not to"

One day last week when wee Johnny came home from school he saw a car parked outside his house and as soon as he saw it he knew the car belonged to a friend of his Mammy's. Johnny was always glad to see her because she brought a present whenever she came. When Johnny got into the house he shook hands with the visitor and then she gave him a parcel. It was a lovely big box of chocolates and Johnny opened it and passed it round twice. The third time his Mammy said, "Put the lid on the box now and leave it on the table. We must keep some for later". Before long the visitor said she had to go and so Johnny's Mammy went out to see her off. Johnny was left alone in the room with the box of chocolates. He went over and opened the box. He was trying to decide which he would take when he was allowed to have one. Then a wee voice inside said, "Take one now Johnny". But Johnny shook his head. "Go on Johnny", said the voice, "There's no one to see and it will never be missed". But Johnny shook his head again. Just then his Mammy came back - she saw the box open - "Johnny", she said, "I hope you're not trying to take a sweet without asking". "Indeed I am not", said Johnny, 'I'm trying very hard not to take one without asking".

You know that is the only way to fight against temptation. Will you remember Johnny and the chocolates the next time that little voice tells you to do something you know you shouldn't do? Try very hard not to.

(Temptation: James ch. 4 v. 7)

TEMPTATIONS
CHOCS

William III

Boys and girls you all know that Friday was the 12th of July, the day which remembers the victory of King William III at the Battle of the Boyne. I would like to tell you the story of William III. It's not about King William but about a boy called William who was at a boarding school. He was given his own desk at school and one of the first things he did was to put on it, with a drawing pin , a little card with William III written on it. All the other boys were very curious to know what it meant and one day they gathered around him and he told them the story of William III. "When I came to school it was the first time I had been away from home. On the day I left, my father took me aside and said, 'There is something I want you always to remember. I want you to try always to put God first, other people second and yourself third'. So William kept the little card on his desk to remind him of his father's advice.

God - 1st; Others - 2nd; Yourself - 3rd - William III. William the Third.

That was very good advice and I would like all the boys and girls to remember it and put it into practice. I don't know how you will remember it. Wee Johnny might print Johnny III on his card, but however you do it, always try to put God 1st, Others 2nd, Yourself 3rd.

(The Twelfth of July)

How a hen sleeps

Wee Johnny's Mammy kept some hens in a house at the bottom of the garden. Johnny was very interested in the way the hens slept at night. Sometimes he slipped in to the house after dark and there they were, all in rows on their roosts. Johnny wondered how they could sleep like that and not fall off. You would think that when they fall asleep they would loosen their grip and topple down. Johnny decided to ask his Daddy how a hen could stay on its perch all night. What was the secret? His Daddy explained to him that when a hen bends its knees it closes its claws so when a hen goes to roost it sits down with its knees bent. So long as it stays like that its claws grip the perch and it can't fall off. "Oh", said Johnny, "the secret of the bended knee".

What lesson can we learn from the hen on the roost. Well there are some things we need to hold on to in life, things like character, love and truth. It's so easy to lose our grip on them. But the secret is the bended knee - that just means prayer. God will give you the power to hold on to what is good. If you forget to pray you will lose your grip and these good things will slip away from you. This is the lesson we learn from the hen - the power of the bended knee, the power of prayer.

And so boys and girls make up your minds to say your prayers every day and you will find that is the secret of a happy life.

(Prayer: Luke ch. 18 v. 1)

Just by chance?

Boys and girls, how many of you know the name of the boy who is remembered in history as the boy who never told a lie. Isn't that a lovely way to be remembered. His name was George Washington and he was the first President of the United States.

One day, when he was a boy, he walked out into the garden at his home and he noticed a very peculiar thing. It was the Springtime and he saw a whole lot of little plants that were just peeping their heads above the ground. But the strange thing was that they weren't just growing in an untidy bunch. When George Washington looked at them he saw that they were coming up to form the letters of his own name - 'George Washington'. He looked at it in amazement for a moment and then he rushed into the house. "Daddy", he shouted, "come quickly and see what has happened". "What is it?" asked his Daddy and George took him by the hand and brought him out into the garden.

"Just look at that", he said as he pointed to his own name, spelled out on the ground. "How very strange", said his Daddy. "But who did it?" said George. "Do you think they could have grown like that by chance?" said his Daddy. "Oh no", said George, "They couldn't possibly have grown like that unless someone had planted them like that". "That's right", said his Daddy, "I planted them because I wanted to teach you a lesson. The lesson is that nothing happens in this world by chance. There is someone who plans everything".

That, boys and girls, is a lesson I would like you all to learn and take to your hearts. Nothing happens in this world by chance. There is no such thing as good luck or bad luck.

(God's Sovereignty: Romans ch. 8 v. 28)

But God in His wisdom is working out His purpose for the world. All things work together for good to them that love God.

Eggs

Boys and girls, how many of you got an egg for breakfast? In wee Johnny's house his Mammy announced, "It's Easter Day. We are going to have boiled eggs for breakfast".

She asked Johnny's Daddy, "How would you like your egg done?" "Soft please", said his Daddy. But Johnny said, "I would like mine done with another one please". Well, Easter is the time for eggs. I'm sure most of you have had a chocolate Easter egg, perhaps with sweets inside.

I have got some eggs with me this morning which I would like to show you. This is a Swan's egg.* Did you ever see one like this? - It is an Emu's egg. And could you believe that this is a real egg. What kind of an egg do you think it is? It's an Ostrich egg. I think one of these would have been enough for Johnny's breakfast, even on Easter day.

There's another egg I would like to show you but unfortunately it got broken. I didn't break it. Although I can't show it to you, I think you know it because it's the most famous egg in the world. You all know its name - Humpty Dumpty.

Humpty Dumpty sat on a wall,
Humpty Dumpty had a great fall,
All the King's horses
And all the King's men
Couldn't put Humpty together again.

Did you know that we are all like Humpty Dumpty? Well, we are, because we have all fallen and been broken by sin. But we are more fortunate than Humpty Dumpty for we have the King himself to help us - King Jesus. God sent His Son Jesus who lived and died and rose again to help us. So although like Humpty Dumpty we may have fallen and been broken in pieces, yet if we love God and open our hearts to Christ the King, we can be made perfectly whole.

**(More readily available eggs e.g. a duck's, could be substituted).*

(New Creation, Easter: 2 Corinthians ch. 5 v. 17)

A boy's New Testament

This is a true story of a little boy who was asked by his mother if he would like to put some money into a mission box. He said, "No, because I'm not sure my money would be used by a missionary". "Well", said his Mammy, "let's buy a New Testament and we'll post it ourselves, straight to a missionary " .

So the boy and his Mammy bought a New Testament. She got the name and address of a missionary in India from the Church magazine. They wrote the boy's name and address inside the New Testament and posted it to India. When it arrived, the missionary gave it to an Indian man from one of the villages. He could speak English and had travelled a great distance through the bush to see the missionary and ask him to come to his village. The missionary was unable to go so the man returned home with the New Testament.

Twenty years later another missionary set out into the bush to preach to people who had not heard of Jesus. When he came to the village I have told you about, the missionary was surprised to be welcomed with great joy by the people. They were obviously delighted to see him and explained that when the New Testament had been brought to them many years before, they had read it and studied it and had met together and formed a Church. The missionary asked to see the New Testament and when he saw the name and address inside, he wrote and told the person what had happened. The boy was now a man and he was so pleased when he got the letter, because he was a Christian and a Sunday School teacher. He always loved to tell the amazing story of how he had helped to build a Christian Church in India, although he himself had never been away from home.

This is the kind of thing any of us might do through the grace and the power of God.

(Missionary Work: Matthew ch. 13 vs. 31, 32)

Who was the wee boy?

One day wee Johnny came home from school with a black eye. When his Mammy saw him she said, "Surely, Johnny you haven't been fighting again". "Well now", said Johnny, "it was like this. I was coming home from school and when I came to the end of the road there was a fight. Big Jimmy Jones was hammering a wee boy much smaller than himself and I only tried to stop him".

"Well that was very brave of you", said his Mammy, "And who was the wee boy?" There was a pause for a moment and then Johnny said, "The wee boy was me".

I wonder, boys and girls, do you see anything wrong with that story? You see, you couldn't say Johnny had told a lie but if his Mammy hadn't asked who the wee boy was, she would never have known that Johnny was quarrelling himself. She would have been deceived.

There are a whole lot of people who would not like t tell a direct lie but who do not hesitate to mislead others. I hope you will never be like that. Remember that God looks beyond our words and our actions, right into our hearts.

Be not deceived, God is not mocked.

(Lies: Exodus ch. 20 v. 16)

Johnny's boat

Johnny was very fond of boats and when he went to the seaside or to visit Lough Erne he always loved to study all the different boats. At home he would carve pieces of wood and make little boats for himself. On his birthday he got a new pen knife and so he started to carve a sailing yacht. It took him a long time but at last it was finished, complete with mast, sails and flag. Johnny was really pleased with it and his Daddy said he would take him to the lake to try it out. Johnny had a long string fastened to it but with the strong wind, the string broke and the little boat went further and further away. Poor Johnny had lost his boat. He was so disappointed. A few weeks later he was in a little town at the other side of the lake and, to his great surprise, in a shop window he saw his boat for sale. Of course he rushed into the shop and bought the boat. "You're my own wee boat", he said, "First I made you, then I bought you".

What does this story remind us of? Of course it's the story of God and man. God made us in His image but we sinned and broke away from God. But God in His love sent His son Jesus to pay the price for our forgiveness. God says, "You're my own wee boy, my own wee girl, first I made you, then I bought you". That is the measure of God's love for us.

(Redemption: 1 Peter ch. 1 vs. 18, 19)

All different but all alike

Last summer the Moderator of the General Assembly was visiting a number of our congregations in seaside resorts. There were lots of people on holiday and the Moderator took services in Newcastle, Bangor and Portrush.

In Portrush when he was speaking to the boys and girls he took a number of things out of his pockets: - a bunch of keys; a coin; a handkerchief and a pen. "Now", he said to the boys and girls, "as you see, all these things are different but there is one way in which they are all the same. Does anybody know how they are all alike?" he asked.

Quick as lightning wee Johnny shot up his hand. "Please sir, they all belong to you". "Well, what a clever boy", said the Moderator, "You are quite right but how did you know the answer?" he asked. "Please sir", answered Johnny, "I heard you telling it last Sunday at Bangor". Well, there's no answer to that!

Here in Church today there are a lot of boys and girls and you are all different. You have different names and different addresses. You are different ages and different heights and you have different personalities. But there is one way in which you are all the same. What is it? It's not that you all belong to me but that you all belong to God.

How do I know? Well, I know because God made you and as well as that He bought you. We read this in Paul's letter to the Corinthians - "You are not your own, you are bought with a price". And the price God paid for you and me was the gift of His son Jesus who came into the world as a little child at Christmas and who, when he was a man, gave His life for us on the cross. I hope in this new year we will all try to be more worthy of the God whose we are and whom we seek to serve.

(New Year, Creation: Psalm 100 v. 3, 1 Corinthians ch. 6 vs. 19, 20)

U812

Last Sunday we were reading from the Book of Genesis about the Garden of Eden where Adam and Eve ate the forbidden fruit. When wee Johnny got home from Church he asked his Mammy and Daddy a riddle - "What happened to the first apple in the world?" When his Mammy and Daddy gave up, Johnny said, "Well, the first apple was eaten by the first pair". Then his Daddy asked Johnny a riddle. "If Adam had had a motor car what would the number have been?"

"That's easy", said Johnny, "Number 1". "That's not right", said his Daddy, "The number of Adam's car would have been U812".

That number carries us back to the story of the forbidden fruit and the fall of man in the Garden of Eden. The whole point in the answer to this riddle is that Adam wasn't alone in his sin. Because he ate the forbidden fruit and fell into sin, all of us fell with him - U812.

You remember the question in the catechism - "Did all mankind fall in Adam's first transgression?" The answer is "The covenant being made with Adam not only for himself but for his posterity, all mankind descending from him by ordinary generation, sinned in him and fell with him in his first transgression" - that just means U812.

But that's not the end of the story because Jesus came to make amends for Adam's sin and He did this by dying on the cross. So as all of us sinned in Adam, through Christ we can all be forgiven.

(Adam's sin: Romans ch. 5 v. 15)

Johnny goes fishing

Wee Johnny was very fond of fishing so one day there had been some rain and he decided the river would be just right. He got his rod and worms and set out to the river. He started to fish and it wasn't long before he caught a small trout. Beside him there was a man with an expensive rod, flies and a landing net but he wasn't catching any fish. Johnny kept on getting small trout and then he caught a bigger one. To the man's surprise Johnny threw the bigger one back into the river. Johnny kept on catching trout but he only kept the smaller ones and put the bigger ones back into the river. The man asked Johnny why he didn't keep the bigger ones and he said, "Mammy's frying pan is only 6 inches wide". Johnny was missing the best and the biggest of the fish because the frying pan was too small.

There are lots of people like that in life who miss the best and biggest things because their hearts are not big enough. Take the things that Jesus offers - happiness, peace, forgiveness - these are the big things. But how do you get them? You must open your heart to Jesus and ask Him to come in and you will find that He will bring with Him the things that make life happy. Those who are content to go on living with a small heart are like Johnny and the small frying pan. They are missing the best and biggest things in life.

(Commitment: Matthew ch. 22 v. 37)

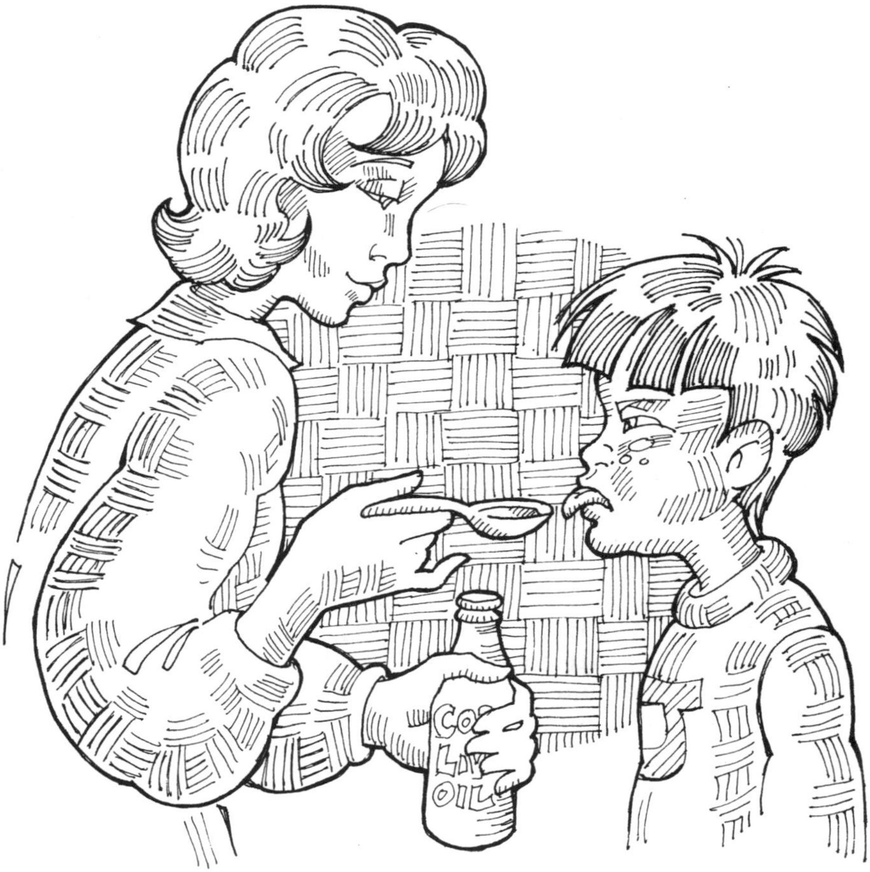
CO
OIL

Johnny's Cod Liver Oil

Boys and girls I hope you have all had a good holiday. You have had a long holiday from school and Sunday School and I hope now you are keen to get back to work. I want you all to do your best to come to Church and Sunday School every Sunday.

I must tell you what happens to wee Johnny when the summer holidays are over and he starts school again. His Mammy buys a big bottle of Cod Liver Oil and Johnny has to take 2 spoonfuls a day. Johnny doesn't like it and he always makes a fuss about taking it. "Why must I take it?" he asks again and again. "Because it's good for you", says his Mammy. "But why is it good for me?" persists Johnny. His Mammy explains to him how the cod fish draws to itself the rays of the sun and stores them in its body and when the oil is extracted it is full of vitamins which are very good for your health. "Well, I don't like it", said Johnny.

That night when Johnny was saying his prayers his Mammy heard him saying, "Please God put all the vitamins in sweets and cake and not in Cod Liver Oil".

Sometimes we think it would be very nice if we could arrange everything to suit ourselves. Maybe it would be, for a while, but when we grow older we begin to discover that the things that we don't like and don't want to do are very often the things that make us happy and content. I hope you'll remember that at home and when you are asked to do something you don't want to do, don't sulk but do it willingly and one day you will understand why life isn't all pleasure. You will see that sometimes, hardship and difficulty lead to success and happiness.

(School year begins; Hardship: Romans ch. 8 v. 28)

Where did they hide Moses?

The lesson in wee Johnny's class in Sunday School was about the Baby Moses. The teacher explained how the Egyptian King decided that all the boy children of the Hebrews should be put to death. The teacher told them how Moses was saved. Wee Johnny listened to the story in Sunday School and when he went home he was all excited. "Do you know where they hid the Baby Moses?" he asked his Mammy. "Where?" she asked. "They hid him in a bull dozer", answered Johnny. Well of course, all you clever boys and girls know that there were no bulldozers when Moses was a baby and that Moses was hidden, not in a bulldozer, but in the bulrushes beside the river. It is a mistake that any of us could make and it shows us the importance of paying attention to what we read and what we are taught. This is very true of what we learn in Sunday School and Church. That is why we are told in the Epistle to the Hebrews. "To give the more earnest heed to the things which we have heard, lest at any time we let them slip". In other words listen carefully in case we forget what we've been told.

(Listening/Ears: Hebrews ch. 2 v. 1; Matthew ch. 13 v. 9)

Riddles

Wee Johnny is very fond of riddles. One night at home he kept asking riddle after riddle but his Mammy and Daddy had heard most of them before and were able to answer them. I expect you know the answers to some of them.

Do you know what has 1 head, 1 foot and 4 legs? - A bed of course.

What do you look for and don't want to find? - A hole in your sock.

What has an eye and can't see? - A needle.

What has an ear and can't hear? - A blade of corn.

"Oh Johnny, we have heard all those before", said his Mammy.

"Well, here's one you'll not guess", said Johnny.

"What has 4 feet, 2 big ears, a nose longer than its tail and flies in the air?" His Mammy and Daddy couldn't guess and had to give up. "An elephant", said Johnny. "But an elephant doesn't fly", said his Daddy. "I know", said Johnny, "I just put that in to make it harder".

I wonder how many of you know what is the hardest riddle of all. We call it the riddle of life. What does life mean? Why are we here? How do you explain things like sorrow, suffering and death?

I don't think anyone can give a complete answer. But certainly pain and sorrow and death are not just put in to make the riddle harder. They all have some purpose in the plans of God. If ever you are puzzled by any of these things that are so hard to explain remember two texts - "God is love" and "All things work together for good to them that love God".

(Sorrow, Pain: 1 John ch. 4 v. 16, Romans ch. 8 v. 28)

Feathers

One day at school wee Johnny "fell out" with one of the boys in his class at school, and Johnny took a spite against him. He started to spread stories about this boy which were not only unkind but untrue. But Johnny couldn't hold spite for long and soon he was sorry for what he had done. He told his Mammy about it and she told him to say he was sorry to the boy in the morning. His Mammy decided to teach Johnny a lesson so when he came home from school his Mammy reached him a brown paper bag tied with a string. It was soft and light and Johnny wondered what was in it. "That's a bag of feathers", said his Mammy, "I want you to take it and go out and put a feather in every garden until the bag is empty". "You're joking", said Johnny, "why do you want me to do that?" "You do it", said his Mammy, "and I'll tell you tomorrow after school why I wanted you to do it". So Johnny did what his Mammy told him and it took him a long time, and he was tired and hungry and a bit cross when he came home.

Next day when he came home from school Johnny said, "Tell me about the feathers?" "Well", said his Mammy, "I want you to take the empty bag and gather up all the feathers you put out yesterday".

"But that's impossible", said Johnny, "The wind has blown them all over the place and I could never find them now".

"That's true", said his Mammy, "I want you to learn a lesson from the feathers. They are just like the stories you told about your friend at school. You may be sorry for them now, but you can never get them back. That's why Jesus said "Every idle word that men shall speak they shall give account thereof in the day of judgment".

So Johnny took the lesson to himself and that night when he was saying his prayers he asked God to help him to never again say anything unkind or untrue about anybody else.

(Gossip: Matthew ch. 12 vs. 36, 37; Psalm 141 v. 3)

The psalmist prayed, "Set a watch O Lord, before my mouth, keep the door of my lips". (Psalm 141 : 3).

The minister's visit

One Sunday in Church the minister announced that he would be visiting during the week in the district where wee Johnny lived. So on Monday wee Johnny's Mammy was busy in the kitchen baking a cake and making some scones. When wee Johnny came home from school he asked if he could have a piece of cake. "No, indeed", said his Mammy, "that cake is for the minister because he is visiting here this week". After that there was a silence for a while and eventually wee Johnny said, "When I grow up I think I'll be a minister". "What makes you think that"? asked his Mammy. "Well", came the answer, "look at all the nice things a minister gets to eat". Then his mother explained that the life of a minister wasn't all tea and cake; there was very much more to it than that.

(The call of God)

But apart from tea and cake I wonder if there is a boy (or girl) in Church today who would like to be a minister or a missionary nurse, doctor or teacher. What a great joy it would be to me if some of the young people in this congregation would hear the call of God and give their lives to His service. I hope all the boys and girls will think about this when you are deciding what to do with your life. For although there are many different ways in which you can serve God, I do hope some of you will hear the call to full time service in the cause of Christ.

David and Goliath

I am sure all the boys and girls know the story of David and Goliath from 1st Samuel. It has always been a great favourite with young people. There is something fascinating about a wee boy from the country fighting and defeating the Giant Goliath.

I want to tell you a story about David which is not recorded in the Bible. You remember how he came up to the battle front to bring food for his brothers who were in the army. When he arrived he found the whole army from Israel disheartened. The Philistines discovered the Giant Goliath and had trained him for battle. Then they issued a challenge to anyone to fight him.

The soldiers of Israel were all afraid, so young David volunteered to fight the giant. Of course they laughed at him. He was so small and not even a soldier, only a shepherd boy from the hills. They told him stories about Goliath. He was so strong and big that David would have no chance at all.

But David was not to be discouraged..He listened quietly to their stories about the size of the giant and then he said, "If he's as big as all that I just couldn't miss him". So he fought and killed Goliath..

That is the spirit with which we should meet all the difficulties of life. If ever you are faced by any task which seems to be beyond you - or any temptation which seems to be too much for you - remember David. Remember especially the secret of his confidence and his strength.

He believed in God and trusted in God and in God's name he fought and won. That is the secret of every victory in life. If you have the faith of David in your heart you will not be discouraged, for with God beside you there is no giant you can't overcome.

(David and Goliath: 1 Samuel ch. 17)

(Impossibilities: Matthew ch. 19 v. 26; Philippians ch. 4 v. 13)

Judge not

One night wee Johnny and his Daddy were coming home and it was a frosty night with snow on the ground. The roads were very slippery and when they came to a steep hill the wheels began to spin and they got stuck half way up. They tried a number of times to get started again but without success. Then they heard a car coming and Johnny's Daddy signalled to it to stop. There was a crowd of young people in it and it just drove on. Johnny said some very unkind things about them and his Daddy had some thoughts about how selfish and inconsiderate young people can be. But when the car reached the top of the hill it stopped and the doors open. Out hopped three boys and three girls. The were going to a dance and although they were all dressed up they walked down the hill in the snow.

"We didn't stop when we were passing or we wouldn't have got started again", they explained. With their help they soon got Johnny and his Daddy going again on their way home. "Well", said Johnny, feeling sorry for the things he had said, "what do you think about that Daddy?" "I certainly learned a lesson to-night Johnny", said his Daddy, "And that is to remember the wisdom of the words of Jesus - 'Judge Not'".

(Judging others: Matthew ch. 7 v. 1)

The baker and the grocer

Once upon a time, a baker and a grocer made a bargain. The grocer needed bread for his shop and the baker needed sugar to put in his cakes. So they decided to swap bread for sugar, pound for pound, one pound loaf of bread for one pound bag of sugar. This arrangement worked well for some time until, one day, the baker thought that the grocer's bag of sugar was not as big looking as it ought to be. So he took one of the bags and weighed it and discovered it was 2 ozs. short.

He thought perhaps the grocer had been in a hurry and had made a mistake. But the next day he weighed it again, and again it was 2 ozs. underweight. So he took a bag of sugar into the grocer's and he said, "You know, this sugar of yours is not the right weight". Then he set it on the scales on the counter and put on a pound weight on the other side.

"Wait a minute", said the grocer, "that's not the way I weigh it". The grocer took off the pound weight and in its place he put one of the baker's loaves and sure enough, they balanced each other perfectly. "You see", said the grocer, "my sugar and your bread are both exactly the same weight and if the sugar is smaller, the loaf must be lighter". The baker went home that day a humbler man. And as he walked back he remembered the words of Jesus. "With what measure ye mete, it shall be measured to you again". There and then, he made up his mind that never again would he do anything dishonest.

(Cheating / Honesty: Matthew ch. 7 v. 2b)

Models

Boys and girls I wonder what you do for a hobby? There are all sorts of things that people do for a hobby. Some people collect all kinds of things - stamps, coins, birds' eggs, wild flowers. Some boys and girls have more active hobbies like swimming, climbing or sailing. Wee Johnny's hobby was making models - especially of aeroplanes or motor cars.

His Daddy often helped him to make these models and he had quite a collection of them. It's hard to imagine Johnny being patient enough to spend time on such detail but it's wonderful what you can do if you are really interested. One day at home wee Johnny was very busy helping his Mammy in any way he could. At night when he was going to bed his Mammy said to him, "Thank you Johnny for all you have done today. You know you're just a model boy". A model boy. Johnny liked that and the next day he looked the word "model" up in the dictionary. It said: "a model is a small imitation of the real thing".

Today boys and girls I might suggest a new hobby for you - making a model, a small imitation of the real thing, making yourself a model of Jesus. What would be better than that, a boy or girl who in every action, word and thought is a model of Jesus, because that, after all, is the purpose of life.

(Making a model: Ephesians ch. 5 v. 1; 1 Thessalonians ch. 1 v. 6)

INSTRUCTION
LEAFLET
DELUXE MODEL
GLUE

Father's day

I wonder how many of you did what wee Johnny did yesterday? What do you think he did? He went shopping. There was something he wanted to buy and he wanted to keep it a secret. Can you guess what it was? If you did what Johnny did you'll know at once. He bought this card. It's a Father's Day card. And on it there is a picture of a man driving along a road in a very sporty car. There is a nice verse inside and Johnny wrote "Love from Johnny" in his best writing. How many of you remembered it was Father's Day? Johnny remembered because he loves and respects his Daddy and he was looking forward to this day. To Johnny there is nobody in the world like his Daddy.

One day Johnny and his best friend began to argue about something. Johnny said it was right. Jimmy said it was wrong and so they argued on. Then Johnny said, "It couldn't be wrong because my Daddy says it's right and if he says it's right, it is right, even if it's wrong".

Well, maybe Johnny took it too far when he said that. But Johnny is obedient. And that's how you can best show your love for your father. And what better day could you begin to do that than today - on Father's Day.

Remember, that if you do that, you will be following the example of Jesus. Jesus loved and honoured his father - Joseph. And also his Heavenly Father. That's how Jesus taught us to think of God as our Father in heaven. He loves everyone with a Father's love and, in return, He asks for our love and obedience.

(Father's Day: Exodus ch. 20 v. 12; Ephesians ch. 6 vs. 1-3)

Twelfth of July - Johnny's telegram

On the Twelfth of July, when we were busy in the church hall feeding the crowds, I was surprised at the number of young people who came to help and most of them worked very hard indeed. There seemed to be no limit to their energy. When I saw it I thought of the feeding of the five thousand and the words of Andrew "There is a lad here". You remember it was a little boy who gave his lunch to Jesus and made this miracle possible. "There is a lad here". But on the 12th there was one lad who wasn't there and we all missed him - wee Johnny. Of course wee Johnny would have been there, only he was away on holidays. When we were ready to serve our first customers a telegram boy came into the hall and gave me a telegram. It had been handed in at 9 o'clock at a Post Office in London and this is what it said - "Hope you have a pushing, rushing, crushing, fussing twelfth of July" and it was signed, "Wee Johnny". Well that's just what we had! Wasn't it very thoughtful of Johnny to remember us. You know there are some people who go away and forget all about the people at home and that's not a good thing. I hope none of you will be like that. I hope when you go away you will always remember those at home who love you and care for you. And, above all, wherever you are, I hope you will never forget the church of your childhood. The church needs you and your help. I hope you will always be ready to do what you can in service to God and His kingdom in the world.

(July, 12th)

Putting the emphasis in the right place

One day at school, wee Johnny's English teacher had some strange sentences for the boys and girls to write.

"Can you write a sentence with 5 'Ands' in a row?" she said. The boys and girls thought and thought but then they gave up. So the teacher told them:-

"A painter was painting a sign 'FISH AND CHIPS' and when he had finished, the owner of the shop looked at it and said, "There is too big a space between 'Fish' and 'And' and 'And' and 'Chips'". That's a sentence with five"Ands' in a row".

Then the teacher said, "There are sentences which are not hard to write but very hard to read. Can you make sense of this sentence?" - 'It was and I said not but'. It makes sense when you put the emphasis in the right place. It was 'AND' I said 'NOT' 'BUT'. Try this on your friends. The whole secret is to know where to put the emphasis.

And so boys and girls it is just the same in life. Some boys and girls emphasise fun and games and neglect their lessons, others behave well with companions but are not so good at home, some think only of what they can get - not what they can give. I hope you will learn what is really important in life and put the emphasis on those things.

Learn to love and respect God and God's house, God's book and God's day. Learn to give your school, your home and your parents the honour they deserve.

Learn to think more of service than money and reward. Then you will be putting the emphasis in the right place and you will be able to make sense of life.

(Priorities: Matthew ch. 6 v. 33)

Whose miserable sub-scription is this?

One Sunday, in wee Johnny's Sunday School class, the story was about the Pharisees asking Jesus if it was lawful to pay tribute to Caesar. The teacher explained that this was a difficult question, so before Jesus answered he asked them for a penny. The teacher explained that, just as our coins have the Queen's head on one side, so the Roman coins in Jesus' day had Caesar's head on one side. Then Jesus held the penny up and said, "Whose image and superscription is this?" They said, "Caesar's" and Jesus told them to render to Caesar the things that are Caesar's and to God the things that are God's.

"Now", said the teacher, "I'll ask you some questions in turn to see if you were listening".

"What was the name of the Roman king in days of Jesus?" - Caesar.

"Who asked Jesus about paying tribute to him?" - The Pharisees.

"What did Jesus do?" - He asked for a penny and held it up.

Then came wee Johnny's turn to answer and his question was, "What question did Jesus ask the Pharisees?" Wee Johnny got a bit mixed up and he said, "Jesus held up a penny and said, 'Whose miserable subscription is this?' "

Although he didn't get it right it was a very sensible answer. Johnny knew a penny wasn't good and yet there are some people who only give a miserable subscription to church and Sunday school. I hope you are not one of them.

(Money: Matthew ch. 22 vs. 15-21)

Writing out the Lord's Prayer

I was talking to a school teacher once and she told me about an unusual exercise she had given her class to do.

Instead of asking them to write an essay she had asked them to write out the Lord's Prayer. This was a class of boys and girls of ten and eleven years old and I don't think there was anyone who wrote it out correctly. The strange thing was that they all knew the Lord's Prayer to repeat. They were able to make some effort to write down the words, but, quite obviously, very few of them had any idea what the words meant. One boy began like this: - "Our Father in charge in heaven". That, of course is perfectly true, for God is in charge of heaven, but that's not what it says in the Lord's Prayer. Another boy wrote, "Our Father which art in heaven, Harold be Thy name". I remember hearing about a boy in London who wrote "Lead us not into Thames Station", for that was the name of the Police Barracks near where he lived. That is not a bad prayer, but it's not the words Jesus taught us to pray.

During his life, Jesus talked a great deal about prayer. He not only told men what to pray for, but how to pray. He said once, "When ye pray, use not vain repetitions." That means not to keep saying a thing over and over again, like a rhyme, unless you really mean what you are saying. We learn the Lord's Prayer when we are young, but we must try to learn not only the words but the meaning of the words.

If we repeat it without meaning, what we are doing is using vain repetition. I would like you to find the Lord's Prayer today in your Bibles or Hymn Books, read it over and try to understand it. If there is anything you don't understand ask your Mammy or Daddy or Sunday School teacher. It is important to understand what we read but it is a thousand times more important to understand what we pray.

(The Lord's Prayer: Matthew ch. 6 vs. 5-13)

I'll sleep at home at night

One day in school, the teacher was asking the class what they were going to do when they left school.

One was going to be a doctor, another a teacher, one a nurse, one a farmer and so on. Wee Johnny and his pal Jimmy were sitting in the back seat and when they were asked, they both said they were going to be sailors. They wanted to sail round the world and see all sorts of strange places. Johnny began to think about this and he thought it would be lovely to travel all round the world but he wanted to sleep at home at night. Poor Johnny. He wanted the thrill of a sailor's life but he also wanted the comfort of his own home and he just couldn't have both. There are a whole lot of things like that in life and Jesus went to great trouble to tell us that. You remember he said "No man can serve two masters for either he will hate the one and love the other or else he will hold to the one and despise the other - ye cannot serve God and Mammon". But the wonderful thing about Jesus is this, that whatever you have to give up to serve Him is not to be compared with all that He gives you in return. When you decide to follow Jesus, you make the wisest and happiest decision of your life.

(Decisions: Matthew ch. 6 v. 24)

Johnny's tidy case

Boys and girls did you have a good holiday? - Wee Johnny had a great time. He was away for a week, camping out with the Boys' Brigade. One night before he went away he brought home a list of things he was to take to camp and he gave it to his mother. A change of clothing, a pair of pyjamas, tooth paste, towels, soap, bathing togs, a hymn book and a Bible. The night before he went off, all the things were collected and set out on the kitchen table. Then Johnny went off to bed and left his mother to pack his case. But like most mothers she put in a few extra things - things she knew Johnny would like. Down at the bottom of the case she put a packet of sweets, a bar of chocolate, some apples and a fruit cake which she had made that afternoon. "What a nice surprise it will be for him when he unpacks his things", she said to herself. Then she folded his clothes neatly and packed them into the case.

Next day Johnny went off to camp and there, for a week, he had a wonderful time. When he came home again he was as brown as a berry, but he wasn't just as tidy as the day he went away.

He looked as if he hadn't washed for a week. There were holes in his socks and his trousers were torn. "What an untidy boy", said his Mammy. "You must not say that", said Johnny, "for I was the tidiest boy in the camp". "You see", said Johnny, "this morning, when we were leaving, the Captain gave a prize for the boy whose case was packed the neatest and I won the prize". "Well I can't understand that", said his Mammy, "for you could never pack a case". "You remember", said Johnny, "how well you packed it when I was leaving. Well I thought it was a pity to disturb it. I never unpacked it and that's how I won the prize". "Poor Johnny", said his Mammy, "if only you had known what was at the bottom of the case". Then she showed him the sweets, the chocolate, the cake and wee Johnny was sorry he had won the prize.

It reminds us of the wonderful provision God makes for us on the journey of life. He surrounds us with his love in Jesus and gives us countless blessings and gifts. But some people never unpack the case and never find the treasures. Boys and girls I hope none of you will make that mistake. Always remember the great goodness of God. Accept with grateful hearts all that he has given and learn to use, with gladness and with thanks, the gifts which he bestows with such a lavish hand.

(God's Provision)

Putting the clock back

Every Sunday wee Johnny has a great rush to get out in time for Sunday School. In his house everyone likes to lie in bed a bit longer on Sunday morning, so Johnny always has to hurry to be in time. Do you know what happened today?

This morning when he got to Sunday School the door was closed. There was nobody about and he just couldn't understand it. So he stood at the door and waited. Then a man came along and smiled at Johnny and said, "Good morning".

"Excuse me", said Johnny, "could you tell me the time please?" "It's just half past nine", said the man and walked on. Then suddenly it dawned on Johnny. They had forgotten to put the clock back and he was at Sunday School a whole hour before the time. Wouldn't it be a great thing, thought Johnny, if they would put the clock back every Saturday night!

I'm sure none of you boys and girls want to put the clock back. When we are young we want to push time on. We want to grow up and get big as quickly as possible. We think the time will never come when we will be old enough to join the Boys' Brigade or the Girls' Brigade. We wish the time would come when we could leave school or learn to drive the car. But I can tell you that as we get older we think differently. We look back and think of all the things we might have done when we were young; all the opportunities we had and didn't take; all the mistakes we made. But no matter how much we may want to do it we can never put back the clock of life. This moment, this hour, this day we never live again. Time never repeats itself. Boys and girls make the most of every opportunity which comes to you when you are young, and what wonderful opportunities there are in the world today. But, above all, try in everything to follow the example of Jesus and as you grow older you will grow in grace.

(Opportunity)

Crossing the Red Sea

One day in Sunday School the lesson in wee Johnny's class was about Moses and the children of Israel and it was from the Book of Exodus. The Exodus means "going out" and this book tells how Moses led the children of Israel out of bondage in Egypt. They were followed by the Egyptian soldiers until they came to the Red Sea. Then when all seemed to be lost God brought about a great deliverance. The teacher read the story from the Bible and then she asked them all questions. One of the questions was "What was the first thing the children of Israel did when they came out of the Red Sea?" Nobody seemed to know the answer but wee Johnny had just come home from holidays where he had been bathing so he said, "Please Miss, they dried themselves and went for a quick run along the beach".

Well it was worth a try, but of course it wasn't right. Johnny should have known better for the whole point of the story is that the children of Israel crossed the Red Sea as a dry land, so of course they weren't wet at all. What they did do when they came out of the Red Sea was to say thanks to God for delivering them from the Egyptian army and they did it in a lovely way. They thanked God in a song of praise. That's what we are going to do now. We are going to say thanks to God for all His goodness and His love to us and we are going to do it in a song. Let's sing the hymn:

'Come, children, join to sing
Hallelujah! Amen! -
Loud praise to Christ our King,
Hallelujah! Amen! -
Let all with heart and voice,
Before His throne rejoice;
Praise is His gracious choice:
Hallelujah! Amen!

(Praise: Psalm 92 vs. 1-3)

My spade

When wee Johnny was young he spent a holiday at the seaside. Every day his Mammy took him down to the beach and he spent his time digging in the sand. One day, when he was trying to make a castle, a gentleman noticed him and thought he would help. He went over and with Johnny's spade he made a great big castle with turrets and a moat all round it. For a while wee Johnny looked on not knowing what to make of it. Then, all of a sudden, he burst into tears and ran over to his Mammy. "That man has my spade", sobbed wee Johnny. Poor Johnny! He didn't appreciate what was being done for him, that the gentleman was being kind and helpful.

Did you ever do anything like that? Yes of course you did! Have you ever said, "That's all wrong", when your Mammy or Daddy have tried to help you with your homework or tried to show you how to do something properly and then you go off in a huff. That's just what wee Johnny did. He didn't want the assistance of someone who was able and willing to help him. Try boys and girls not to make that mistake. Learn to appreciate all that people do to help you because they love you. Remember your parents are older and wiser than you are and you'll generally find that they are right after all.

(Parents: Ephesians ch. 6 vs. 1-3)

The Donkey

Boys and girls do you know the story about the animals that went to school? There were six of them - an elephant, a donkey, a pig, a monkey, a dog and a cat - I'm sure it was a very noisy class.

What do you think was the first thing they had to do? Believe it or not, it was an intelligence test! To find out which animal was the cleverest they had to do a lot of practical tests. I'm sure you can all guess who came out top. First was the monkey, 2nd the dog, 3rd the cat, 4th the elephant, 5th the pig, 6th the donkey. The donkey was the bottom of the class. None of us gives the donkey much credit for being clever. "As stupid as an ass" we say. If anyone ever calls you "a stupid ass" I hope you won't be ashamed or annoyed. Although a donkey is thought to be stupid, nonetheless it once had a most important task to fulfil. On the Sunday before Jesus was crucified, He entered the City of Jerusalem, not on a chariot with an escort of soldiers, but riding on a donkey. The people waved palm branches in the air and shouted "Hosanna to the King". And so the donkey had its great day. The next time you see a donkey, think about this. He wasn't very clever or intelligent but he had an important part to play in helping Jesus.

Although we all like to be clever, never forget there are many far more important things in life. The most important is to learn to help others and above all to help Jesus.

(Palm Sunday: 1Cor. ch. 1, vs. 26-29)

How Johnny and Reuben spent Christmas

One day wee Johnny and a little Jewish boy called Reuben were having a chat about Christmas. Johnny was talking all about what he was going to get from Santa and how he would spend Christmas Day. Johnny said that when he woke up on Christmas morning he would open all the parcels Santa brought and he would play with the toys until it was time to get ready for church. "When we come back from church", Johnny continued, "Mammy will make the Christmas dinner and after that we'll have lots of presents to open under the Christmas tree from all our friends. We'll play with our toys all afternoon and later we'll go to visit our cousins. We'll take our toys with us to show to them and they'll show us all their toys and we'll have great fun". Then Johnny said to Reuben, "How will you spend Christmas?" Reuben said, "Jews don't believe in Christmas so on Christmas Day my Daddy and I will go to our toy factory. We'll look at all the empty shelves and count all the money we have made from selling our toys and then we'll sing 'What a friend we have in Jesus'".

Boys and girls I hope you can all sing "What a friend we have in Jesus", but not for the same reason as Reuben and his dad. I hope you can sing it because you know Jesus as Saviour and Friend and someone who loves you and wants to help you.

(Christmas)

"Pig-Pig"

One day wee Johnny was out in the car with his Daddy. They were driving along a wee country road. It was narrow and twisty and they had to drive slowly. "You need to be careful on a road like this", said his Daddy, "You never know what's round the corner, so you must keep alert and be ready to stop". The words were hardly out of his mouth when they saw a car coming round the corner in front of them. They slowed down and kept well into their own side of the road. The other car did the same.

"Watch out", said Johnny, "it's a lady driver". As the two cars met the lady opened her window and shouted at his Daddy, "Pig", she shouted, "Pig". "What's wrong with her?" said Johnny. "I don't know", said his Daddy, "I couldn't have given her any more room". "Well she's all worked up about something", said Johnny and it wasn't long until they knew the reason! What do you think it was? As they came around the corner, right in front of them, in the middle of the road - what do you think? A pig.

"There you are", said Johnny, "There wasn't anything wrong with the lady. She was only trying to be helpful". "Well I hope you'll learn a lesson from the pig", said his Daddy. "What do you mean?" asked Johnny. "It's like this", said his Daddy, "As we travel the road of life we meet many people who are older and wiser than we are because they have travelled the road before us. They know its hidden dangers and sometimes they warn us to be careful. But, just like that lady, often they are misunderstood. We think there is something wrong with them when they warn us to be careful and all the time they are only trying to be helpful". Just then they met another car and as they passed Johnny shouted, "Pig! Pig! I hope he is careful", he added. "Yes ", said his Daddy, "and I hope you will remember that pig the next time you are warned about something you shouldn't do".

(Warnings/ Misunderstanding: Proverbs ch. 1 v. 8)

Johnny's new uniform

For some time wee Johnny has been saving up for something he wanted to buy. It was his Lifeboy uniform. So every penny he got was put away in a box. He was always looking for things to do so that he could earn some money. Every now and then he counted his money and with some help from his Mammy he soon had enough to buy the uniform. He brought his money to his Lifeboy Leader. There were six boys getting new uniforms and the leader said that he would have them for the next night. Johnny could hardly wait a whole week until the Lifeboy night. The six new Lifeboys got their uniforms and when they put them on they were very proud of themselves. "Now remember", said the Leader, "When you wear your uniform everybody judges the Lifeboys by what they see you do, so never do anything when you are in uniform that would bring dishonour to the great Boys' Brigade Movement". It was very good advice and the boys all listened attentively.

Johnny rushed home to show his uniform to his Mammy and she said, "It's a lovely uniform, you'll have to be very good to it". "I know", said Johnny, "and I'll have to be very good when I'm in it because our Leader said that if you are ever tempted to do anything wrong, don't do it until you take off your uniform". "I'm sure that's not what he said", answered his Mammy, "I expect he said if ever you are tempted to do anything wrong - don't do it at all. Anything that is wrong is always wrong no matter what clothes you have on. God judges a person, not by what he wears, but by what he is".

Boys and girls you should never do anything that would bring dishonour to yourself or to the uniform of any organisation to which you belong. If you are tempted ask God to help you, ask Him to give you the power to resist. It tells us in the Epistle of James "Resist the devil and he will flee from you".

(Temptation: James ch. 4 v. 7)

Church

Last Christmas the teacher asked wee Johnny to paint a text for her. It was to hang at the back of the stage during the Christmas play. The teacher gave Johnny a roll of paper to take home. She told him the text and the size he was to paint it. But when he thought about starting Johnny couldn't remember either the text or the size.

"Please Mammy", he pleaded, "you ring the teacher and ask her". When she came back from the phone she was laughing - "The text, Johnny, is 'Unto us a child is born' and it's 8 feet long and 2 feet wide".

Well, your text is not as big as that. It is just one word and it is written over fifty times in the New Testament. It is the word 'Church'. The word church can mean a number of different things but I want you to think of it today as the place where the followers of Jesus meet to worship God. Of course we can worship God at any time or in any place but the Bible calls us to meet together to worship. Early Christians met in each other's houses, then later meeting houses or churches were built to worship together. The people treated these buildings with reverence and respect because they were coming to God's house. Now, I wonder how many different things you can think of which we do when we come to church? The hymn we are going to sing "We love the place O Lord, wherein thine honour dwells" mentions 3 different things we do in our worship.

Firstly, "It is the house of prayer" - this is one of the most important parts of our worship - prayer. This is how we speak to God and He speaks to us.

Secondly, "We love the word of life", says the hymn. This means the word of God - the Bible. As we read it in worship we can hear God speaking to us.

Prayer, reading and thirdly, "We love to sing", says the hymn. We sing when we are happy and because we have found happiness in Jesus. We sing hymns and psalms in our worship.

Jesus loved the boys and girls and called them into His Church. This is the message I want to leave with you today. 'Church' - but if you are (ur) missing the church is not complete CH(UR)CH. Never forget UR needed in the church.

(Hymn "We love the place O God"; Church)

Johnny's five pound note

One time wee Johnny was away at camp with the Boys' Brigade. Two or three days after they arrived one of the boys was sent to the Post Office to see if there were any letters for the camp. Amongst the bundle of letters there was one for wee Johnny. He opened it excitedly, looked what was inside and then put it in his pocket. It didn't take him a minute and when Johnny's friend had finished his letter he said to him, "Any news from home?" "Oh yes", said Johnny, "I had a note from Daddy. It said he was well and he wished me a very happy time at camp and told me that he loved me". "It couldn't have been much of a letter", said Johnny's friend, "for it didn't take you long to read it". "It wasn't a letter at all", said Johnny, "it was just a note. You see it was a five pound note".

Although it didn't say much it was enough to tell Johnny that his Daddy was well and he knew from the gift that his Daddy wished him a good time and that he loved him. Surely that's the very thing we can all learn from life. When we think of all the gifts which we receive every day, and all the things that are provided to make us happy we know that our Father in Heaven really loves and cares for us. We should never forget that God is the giver of all good things, and we should learn to love Him in return for His great love to us.

(Providence: James ch. 1 v. 17)

"...how I am getting on"

I don't think I told you that wee Johnny got a job as a message boy during the Christmas holidays. One day in the paper he saw an advertisement saying, "Wanted a smart boy to do messages during the Christmas holidays". Well wee Johnny answered the advertisement and he got the job.

One night, a few days after he had started, he phoned his new boss. Without saying who he was he said he had seen the advert in the paper and he asked if the job was still vacant. "Oh no", said his boss, "we already have got someone and he's doing very well". And wee Johnny just couldn't hold back any longer. "Thank you, thank you", he said, "This is wee Johnny speaking and I was just phoning up to see how I am getting on".

You know that's not a bad thing to do. It tells us in the Bible "Let a man examine himself" and that's what we should all do in the presence of God. Ask Him how you are getting on and if there is anything wrong that needs to be put right. Ask Him to help you and you will find that He is always willing and able to do just that.

(Self-examination: Psalm 139 vs. 23, 24; 1 Corinthians ch. 11 v. 28)

No parades on the Twelfth

One evening wee Johnny came into the house, all serious and as excited as could be. His Daddy was watching something on television. His Mammy was knitting and his sister was reading a book. No one took any notice of Johnny. "Do you know what I heard when I was out?" said Johnny and they all looked at him. "There are going to be no parades on the Twelfth". That made them sit up! His Daddy turned off the T.V., his Mammy put down her knitting and his sister closed her book. "Who told you?" said his Daddy. "Oh, it's right enough", answered Johnny, "There are going to be no parades on the Twelfth". "And why not?" asked his Daddy, full of interest. They all waited to hear why. Then Johnny said, "Because the Twelfth is on a Sunday and the parade will be on the 13th".

Of course it was only a trick Johnny was playing and there's no harm in it. But I want you to think about this because it can teach us a lesson. "There are going to be no parades on the Twelfth". That of course was true as far as it went but the point is, it wasn't the whole truth. There was deception in the way Johnny told it, as if it was some startling news. You see how easy it is to deceive people even when you tell the truth or part of the truth.

A witness in court has to promise to the truth, the whole truth and nothing but the truth.

We should always be very careful in life to do just that. It means that when you say anything you will not keep something back or add anything to try to deceive others. James wrote in his Epistle "Let your yea be yea and your nay, nay". If you do that you will be what every follower of Jesus should be - a person whose word is his bond.

(Truth, The Twelfth of July: James ch. 5 v. 12)

God needs us now

One day wee Johnny and his friend Jimmy were having a very serious talk. They were thinking of the future and painting great pictures in their imagination. Johnny was going to do this and Jimmy was going to do that. But they agreed that, whatever happened, they would always be friends.

Then as a test of their friendship Jimmy said, "If you had £2,000 would you give me £1,000?". "I would indeed, gladly", said Johnny. "If I had £200 would you give me £100?" "I certainly would", said Johnny. "If you had two 10p pieces would you give me one?" There was a pause and then Johnny said, "I'd need to think about that". "Why do you hesitate? If you would share £2,000 or perhaps £200, why should you not share two ten pence pieces?" said Jimmy. "Well, you see", said Johnny, "It just happens that I have two ten pence pieces".

You see there are some people in life who are great at saying what they would do if only they had such and such a thing - how good they would be, how generous, how kind. But sometimes when you show them how they can help at the moment and with what they already have, then suddenly they don't seem so keen to help. That is very true in the service of God. Remember God is depending on what you can give Him now. He needs you now. Don't wait until you grow up or make a fortune.

The time to begin to serve God is today. No matter how young or how poor you may be - God wants you just as you are. If you come to Him today He will make and mould you for His purposes and use you in the service of His Kingdom.

(Serving God - today)

Trust

Johnny wasn't very good about sharing his toys and books with others. He likes to keep all his things to himself. Johnny is afraid that somebody else might be careless with them and destroy them. And while it's a good thing to be careful with your belongings it's a bad thing not to share your things with others. Many a talk Johnny and his Mammy had about it. Somebody wants to borrow something from Johnny and he doesn't want to lend it. "He'll only ruin it", says Johnny when his Mammy says he should lend it. She says, "You must learn to have more faith in your friends, you must learn to trust people Johnny". "Do you always trust me?" asked Johnny. "Of course I do", was the answer. "Then why do you keep the sweets locked up in the cupboard", said Johnny.

That was a hard one to answer but his Mammy explained that sometimes wee boys would eat more than was good for them if they were left to themselves. "It's not that I don't trust you Johnny", said his Mammy, "but there's no use putting temptation in your way". And that's the truth of it. Every time we say the Lord's prayer we pray "Lead us not into temptation" and when God answers that prayer we never think of saying that He doesn't trust us.

So although in your house and mine good things are kept out of sight we should never think our parents don't trust us. They love us and know what is best for us. And so we should trust them in all things and we should try to be worthy of their trust.

(Trust / temptation)

BREAD
HONEY

50,000 thousand Bibles - not to be read

I want to tell you about 50,000 Bibles which were once printed in the hope that they would never be read. Why do you think it was hoped that they would never be read? I'll give you a clue. They were printed by the British and Foreign Bible Society and each one was packed in a special waterproof cover. Now can you guess why? They were packed like that because it was planned to put one in every lifeboat carried by ships in case of shipwreck. So you see why it was hoped they would never be read.

It reminds us that in times of danger, people turn naturally to God and many find comfort, strength and encouragement through reading the Bible. There are millions of people all over the world who read the Bible, not just when they are in danger but every day. What about you? Do you do that?

You remember what Paul said when he wrote to his young friend Timothy - "From a child thou hast known the scriptures which are able to make thee wise unto salvation".

It would be a great joy to me if I could say the same thing about every boy and girl and every man and woman in church today.

(Bible Sunday: 2 Timothy ch. 3 v. 15)

Harvest riddles

Boys and girls I want to ask you three harvest riddles so listen carefully and see if you know the answers.

1. What has ears but can't hear? - corn.
2. What has eyes but can't see? - potatoes.
3. What has a heart but can't love? - a cabbage.

We should all thank God that He has given us ears to hear, eyes to see and hearts to love.

Ears to hear what? Above all to hear God's voice. To do that, we have to be very quiet because God speaks in a still small voice.

Eyes to see what? To see the beauty of God's world, the sky, the sea, the hills, the fields, the trees and the flowers.

Hearts to love? Yes, to love each other and to love God. You remember that Jesus said that the greatest of all the commandments is to love God and to love others.

May your ears be open to hear God's voice, your eyes to see the beauty of His world and, above all, may your heart love God - for all His love to you.

(Harvest: Matthew ch. 22 vs. 37-39)

Johnny's piano practice

Wee Johnny was taking lessons at the piano because his mother had dreams that, one day, he would be a good pianist. But Johnny himself didn't care much whether he would ever be able to play or not. He didn't mind the lessons but he just hated to practise at home. Those endless scales up and down and up and down. If he was allowed to play a decent tune it wouldn't be so bad. One day when he was practising the lady next door came over to speak to his mother. She heard Johnny at the piano and instead of ringing the bell she knocked at the window and shouted to Johnny, "Is your Mammy at home?" "What do you think?" answered Johnny, "do you think I would be sitting here if Mammy was out!"

I'm sure most boys and girls are the same. They don't like doing their lessons or practising the piano. But you know boys and girls, it's a good plan to make yourselves do things you don't like to do. When you get older and get out into the world on your own you will find that you can't just do what you like. You'll often have to do things you don't want to do. The person who gets on in life is the person who does those unpleasant duties with a smile and a cheerful heart.

So even you never learned to play the piano it would be good for you to sit for half an hour every day practising the piano, and the more you dislike it, the more good it does you. Will you remember that when you are asked to do anything at home which you don't want to do? Don't grumble and grouse and complain, but do it with a smile for that will help you some day to be a better man or woman.

(Practice)

Corn doll

Wee Johnny's sister Mary said she would like a doll for Christmas, so their Mammy decided to make Mary a doll. She bought a pattern and a doll's face with curly hair. Very carefully she cut it out and sewed it together. She didn't know what to stuff it with, so Johnny suggested that she use corn grain. He ran out to the barn and brought in enough grain to stuff the doll. When his Mammy had it finished she dressed it and it looked very nice indeed. Mary loved her new doll and she took it everywhere with her. One day wee Johnny and Mary had a big row and in a fit of temper wee Johnny took Mary's doll and buried it in the garden. He never told anyone what he had done and there was a great search for the doll but it wasn't found.

In the spring time Johnny's Daddy was working in the garden and he noticed some fresh green shoots. He thought it looked like corn but wondered how it ever got there. He went over with his spade and began to dig and soon he came on the remains of Mary's doll. The corn with which it had been stuffed had found new life and had started to grow. So at last the mystery of the lost doll was solved. Johnny's secret was discovered. His sin had found him out.

That is what happens in the world of nature every spring time when trees and hedges and seeds begin to bud and grow. It was the same miracle which happened on Easter Day when Jesus who was dead was raised to newness of life by the touch of God. This is what the Resurrection means, that Jesus, who on Good Friday was crucified and put to death at Calvary, was raised up by God on Easter Day and is alive for evermore.

(Easter: Numbers ch. 32 v. 23; 1 Corinthians ch. 15 vs. 37-44)

Give him our Daddy

One day when wee Johnny was away on holiday he was playing on the sands when he came across a little boy playing on his own. He wasn't as well dressed as Johnny, he had no bucket or spade and he had no money for ice cream or sweets. He had no toys to play with but, worst of all, Johnny discovered he had no Daddy. Johnny became friendly with this little boy and he let him play with his ball and cricket bat. They met each morning on the sands and played together. All went well until, one morning, Johnny got out of the wrong side of the bed. All day he was cross and cranky. He wouldn't lend any of his things to his little friend. That night his Mammy talked to him and said, "You should remember Johnny that your little friend has no Daddy to buy him toys, no Daddy to buy him ice cream, no Daddy to buy him a bucket and spade. You should be glad to share what you have with him". "But I don't want to share my toys", said Johnny, "I don't want to give him my things, but if you like you can give him our Daddy".

You see Johnny wanted to keep all the things his father had given him but he was ready to part with his father.

There are lots of people like that in life. They are ready to accept and keep the gifts of God but they refuse to accept the giver. We all take God's gifts but how many of us have room in our hearts for God himself. Never forget that the best way you can show your gratitude to God is just to give your heart to Him. I hope you will all accept God's greatest gift - the gift of Jesus, His Son.

(God's gift - Jesus)

The Rotten Apples

Wee Johnny and some of his friends had really been very naughty. They had done something which they certainly should not have done. Wee Johnny was worried because he knew that if his father found out, he would be punished. He kept hoping that no one had seen them and that they would get away with it this time. Johnny made his way home only to find that someone had told his father. His Daddy said to him, "Johnny, I've heard what has happened and I'm very disappointed". Instead of punishing him his Daddy said, "Go out into the orchard and pull me three of the very best apples you can find". Johnny ran out to find the apples, still wondering why his Daddy had not scolded him. When he brought back the three good apples his father said, "Now go and get me a rotten apple". Johnny did this and his Daddy told him to put the four apples together in the cupboard. A few days later Johnny's father called him to look at the apples and what did they find? Four rotten apples! One bad apple beside three good apples can make them all bad.

"You see Johnny", said his Daddy, "I happen to know that there was a naughty boy with you who had a very bad influence over you all. Please do be very careful the company you keep. Don't be easily led and tempted to do something you know to be wrong".

The Bible warns us that "Bad company ruins good character".

(Bad company: 1 Corinthians ch. 15 v. 33)

Jumble sale Bible

Some time ago I was at a jumble sale. There were all kinds of things to be sold. There were hats, coats, shoes, shirts and ties and I saw one wee boy who had bought a kite. But I want to tell you about an old man who had bought a book. It was a Bible without a back, which somebody had sent to the sale. I was watching and I made my way through the crowd to this old man who had bought the Bible. I asked him if he knew what book he had bought. "Indeed I do", he replied. "It's a Bible". "Well I hope you'll read it", I said. "Indeed I will", said he, "because I believe it's true and what's more", he added, "I try to practise what it teaches".

I never thought I would have learned such a lesson at a jumble sale - for you know it is a lesson we all need to learn, not only to read and believe the Bible but also to practise what it teaches. It would take a lifetime to tell you all the Bible teaches but if we would begin to practise this one central message it would soon transform our land and give us something to be proud of. "Thou shalt love the Lord thy God and thy neighbour as thyself". This is what the Bible teaches - will you try to put it into practice?

(Bible: James ch. 1 v. 22)

Sending messages

Boys and girls have you ever thought how many different ways there are of sending messages? It would be very interesting to sit down some day and make a list. One of the strangest ways and one that is used by boys and girls all over the world at this time of the year is to write a letter and put it up the chimney - you know what I mean. Of course if you were writing to me or one of your friends you wouldn't put it up the chimney. You would put a stamp on it and put it in the pillar box. If you were in a hurry you might you use the telephone.

Sometimes on the radio or on T.V. we hear urgent messages for people who are wanted at once. Scouts and Guides will know another why of sending messages - it's called Morse Code. It can be sent by radio or by flags or even lights. But you don't even need to be able to see or hear or even speak to send messages. Blind people can give messages by Braille and deaf and dumb people can speak to each other by sign language. So you see there are all sorts of ways of sending messages.

But suppose some day you had a very important message to send and you wanted to make sure it was delivered. You would go with it yourself or send someone to deliver it for you. And you know God has all kinds of ways of sending messages to His children. But when He wanted to send the most important message, He sent Jesus His Son. And Jesus brought the message of Good News for you and me and all the world. The news that God so loved the world that He gave His only begotten son, that whosoever believeth on Him should not perish but have everlasting life.

We should rejoice that we have heard this message and remember all those in the world who do not know about the love of God.

(Christmas: John ch. 3 v. 16)

Get it over quickly

I want to tell you about the day wee Johnny went to a strange church. He was staying at his Uncle's house and on Sunday he went to Church with his Uncle. It was the biggest church he had ever been in. In the porch there were a number of men standing to shake hands and welcome people to Church. One of them shook hands with Johnny and welcomed him to Church. Johnny and his Uncle went into Church and when they sat down his Uncle bowed his head. Johnny watched him and thought he was saying a prayer so Johnny bowed his head and said a prayer too.

On the way home after Church they talked about the service and Johnny pointed out all the things that were different from his own Church at home. Then he said to his Uncle, "What did you pray for when you went into Church?" But for an answer his Uncle just asked him the same question - "What did you pray for?" "Well", answered Johnny, "I just prayed, O God get it over quickly".

It was a perfectly honest answer and it expresses the thoughts of a great many people who come to Church and they are not all wee people.

They don't want a long service, they don't want a long sermon, they just want to get it over quickly.

Well I hope you will all learn to say a prayer when you come into Church, not Johnny's prayer but one of your own. Just bow your head and ask God to bless the preacher and the people around you and ask Him to give you a humble and loving heart.

(Prayer)

Deceptive depths

Boys and girls, all day yesterday wee Johnny was having a great time in the floods. He had his wellingtons on and he was out and about early, watching the water rise. He was standing at a place where the water was out on the road. In spite of all the hardship the floods cause to many people, Johnny was enjoying it. Part of the excitement was watching a flock of ducks that were swimming about in the water. When the first car came along it stopped and the driver asked Johnny if the water was deep. "Oh, not at all", said Johnny, "you'll get through it easily". So the car set off but when it got near the middle the water started to come in and the engine stopped. The driver opened the window and shouted back to Johnny, "I thought you said it wasn't deep". "I didn't think it was deep", shouted Johnny, "it's only half way up on the ducks".

You know that's a mistake many people make in life - they think sin is a very shallow thing and easy to pass through. They don't realise how deep it is until they get into the middle and find themselves in difficulty. The wise thing to do whenever we meet the evil floods of life is to stop, to turn back and to ask for God's help to save us from sin.

(Sin)

Picture of God

One night at home wee Johnny hadn't so many lessons to do as usual. When he had them all done he still had an hour before bedtime. So he got some paper and a pencil and he began to draw. His Mammy was busy sewing but she noticed Johnny was very quiet and she wondered what was wrong. "Have you your lessons all finished?" she asked. "Yes", said Johnny. "And what are you doing now?" said his Mammy. "I'm drawing a picture of God", said Johnny. "A picture of God", repeated his Mammy. "You can't draw that, sure nobody knows what God is like". "Ah well", said Johnny, "they'll know when I finish my picture".

Of course Johnny's Mammy wasn't just altogether right when she said that. Nobody knows what God is like and that was one reason why Jesus was born. He came to paint a picture of God. Before Jesus came, you see, for many years men and women had wondered and guessed about what God was like. But Jesus said, "I and my father are one. He that hath seen me hath seen the Father". By His life on earth and His death on the cross, He taught the world that God is love. But Jesus did more than paint a picture. He also gave an example of life at its best and called on all men to follow in His footsteps. Boys and girls when we live like Jesus and are upright and honourable, kind and unselfish, pure and true, we are really painting a picture of God.

That is the great purpose of our life in this world - for all of us are made in the image of God.

(God:
John ch. 10 v. 30
and ch. 14 v. 9)

Johnny.
CRAYONS

The dumb man and the blind man

I want to tell you a story about a dumb man and a blind man. They went into a shop one day, the dumb man wanted a hammer and the blind man wanted a toothbrush. So the dumb man went up to the counter and hit it with his fist as if he were hammering. The man behind the counter knew at once what he wanted and went and got him a hammer. Now I want you to show me what the blind man did to show he wanted a toothbrush.

I see a lot of boys and girls pretending to clean their teeth. But you are wrong. Why? Although the blind man couldn't see, he could talk and he simply said, "I want a toothbrush please". Don't worry if you made a mistake, it's easy to get caught.

Now if God has given us our speech and the gift of sight let us be very thankful. It is important in life to use all the gifts of God, whether we are working with our heads or with our hands, or even playing games with our feet. Whatever we do we should do to the best of our ability and we should do it always to the glory of God.

(Gifts: Colossians ch. 3 v. 17)

Johnny and the fish

Wee Johnny's Daddy liked to go fishing. Although he didn't catch many fish, when he did get any, he shared his catch with his friend who lived in town. Sometimes he would send wee Johnny in with the parcel of fish.

The first time Johnny went, he was very shy and polite. He rang the door bell, waited for someone to answer, then handed in the parcel and said, "Here is some fish from my Daddy". As time went on he got more familiar. He just opened the door and left the parcel on the table in the hall.

Then one day he was in a great hurry, so he walked into the house and pushed open the sitting room door and said, "There's your fish", and banged the parcel down on the table.

But the gentleman thought he would teach Johnny a lesson, so he called him back. He said, "Johnny when you came at first you were quiet and polite. Lately I have noticed you just burst in and rush out again. Now I'll show you how you should deliver your parcel. You sit up here and pretend you are me and I am you". So the gentleman went out and knocked on the door and when Johnny said, "Come in", he opened the door, bowed and said, "Good morning Sir, here is your fish". Then Johnny said, "Thank you and here is 20p for your trouble".

You see that man was able to see the faults of others but didn't see his own faults. We all have plenty of faults and failings of our own without picking holes in others. "Why beholdest thou the mote that is in thy brother's eye, but considerest not the beam that is in thine own eye".

(Fault-finding: Matthew ch. 7 vs. 1-5)

Johnny learns to be a ventriloquist

In one of the books that wee Johnny got for Christmas there was an article about "How to become a ventriloquist" and Johnny had read it over and over again. You know what a ventriloquist is. It is a person who can speak without moving his lips and can make you think the voice is coming from somebody else. Well, wee Johnny thought it would be a great thing if he could do just that. He decided not to tell anybody but every night when he went up to bed he took out his book and stood in front of the mirror and went over the different exercises again and again. Soon he was able to say a few words in a great deep voice without moving his lips.

One night Johnny was watching T.V. and his Mammy said, "Johnny it's time you were in bed. Run up now and when you are in, knock the floor and I'll come up and say good-night". In no time at all his Mammy heard the knock on the floor. "I wondered how you got in so quickly", said his Mammy, "you didn't fold your clothes and I'm sure you didn't say your prayers". "Oh yes", answered Johnny, "I did say my prayers". "Well, it didn't take you long", said his Mammy. "I know", said Johnny, "but I said them all right", and then he closed his eyes and asked, "Didn't I God?" and without moving his lips came the big deep voice, "O yes Johnny, you said your prayers". His Mammy laughed, "I didn't know you were a ventriloquist", she said. So Johnny told her his secret. "Well that's a good one", said his Mammy, "but you made one mistake - when God speaks to us, he speaks with a still small voice and that is why, if you want to hear His voice, you must come to Him with reverence and quietness". It was a lesson Johnny took to his heart and he made up his mind that when he was saying his prayers he would always wait for a moment in stillness to listen to the voice of God.Every

Sunday in Church he wouldn't talk or fidget or do anything to annoy others who were trying to listen to the still small voice.

(Listening to God:
1 Kings
ch. 19 vs. 11-13;
Psalm 85 v. 8)

Black eye for forgiveness

One day wee Johnny was coming home from school with his friend Jimmy. They were walking along together chatting to each other when, all of a sudden, they both made a great dive towards the ground. Do you think you could guess why? They both had seen a 10p piece lying on the footpath and without saying anything to each other they both dived for it. After a bit of a struggle Jimmy got the 10p into his hand and Johnny wasn't too pleased. He said that he had seen it first and so it ought to be his and Jimmy said that he had got it first and was going to keep it. Well they argued for a while and then they began to push each other and finally they started to fight. Before long Johnny had a big black eye. When he got home his Mammy asked what had happened and Johnny told her. Then he said that he would get his own back in the morning. "I'll soon show him he can't do that to me and get away with it".

His Mammy listened and said nothing but that night when he was in bed his Mammy came up, as she always did, to read the Bible and say their prayers together.

She read what Jesus said about people who had quarrelled, how they should forgive each other and be friends.

When she had finished she said, "You know Johnny, you should forgive Jimmy". "I'll forgive him when I get my own back", said Johnny. "You should forgive him now", said his Mammy, "Wouldn't it be terrible if anything happened and you died during the night and you hadn't forgiven Jimmy". That made Johnny think and after a minute he said, "All right, I will forgive him but if I'm still here in the morning, he better look out for himself".

Poor Johnny, he wasn't really ready to for

give Jimmy, for when we forgive we must also forget. I know that's not easy to do but it will help us to remember that Jesus prayed for those who put him to death - "Father, forgive them", prayed Jesus. We should always try to follow the example of Jesus and forgive and forget.

(Forgiving Others: Luke ch. 23 v. 34)

History exam - 100%

One day wee Johnny came home from school and announced that he had had his history exam. "Well, how did you get on?"asked his Mammy. "It was too easy", answered Johnny, "I got 100%".

"Did the teacher give you your marks?" asked his Mammy. "No, not yet", said Johnny, "but I got 100%". "How do you know, if you didn't get your marks", asked his Mammy. "Well you see, there were just two questions and I got them both right", Johnny replied. "The first was - what was the date of the Battle of the Boyne? Imagine asking us a question like that - far too easy! I wrote 1690 and I know that was right. The second question was: What was the date of the Battle of Hastings? I wasn't too sure of the answer so I just wrote 'I don't know' and that was right too". Well I don't know how many marks the teacher gave him but if I had been marking the paper I would have given him full marks, not of course for history, but for his frankness and his common sense.

You know there are some people and they would almost be ashamed to answer "I don't know" to a question. There is an old saying that "the more you know - the more you know you don't know" and it's very true. Even Jesus who knew more about God and the things of God than anybody who ever lived, wasn't ashamed to answer "I don't know".

Remember once He was asked about the end of the world and He answered "Of that day and hour knoweth no man - not even the Son". And so boys and girls, we should use all the brains that God has given us and take every chance to learn all we can. But always remember that it's better, much better, to be honest and truthful than to pretend to be more clever than we really are.

(Second Coming/ Honesty: Matthew ch. 24 v. 36)

Making excuses

I want to tell you a story about a Greek boy who lived long ago. One day he was riding along the road on his donkey. Overhanging the road there were a lot of fruit trees and the fruit was ripe and ready to eat. Every now and then the boy would put up his hand and try to reach the fruit, but it was too high. Then he hit on a great idea. He stopped the donkey and led it over and made it stand under the nicest bunch of fruit he could find. Then carefully he climbed up on its back, stood straight up and caught hold of one of the branches. Just as he did so the donkey moved off and left him hanging from the tree. Just at that moment who should come along but the farmer who owned the fruit. "What are you doing there?" he shouted to the boy. "Please Sir", came the timid reply, "I fell off my donkey".

I wonder what you would have said if you had been in his position. I hope you are not one of those people who are always making excuses for themselves. It is bad enough to make a mistake. We all do that, but it only makes it twice as bad when we tell lies about it and try to makes excuses. The Duke of Wellington once said, "The boy who is good at making excuses is seldom good at anything else". Remember that the next time you make a mistake. Don't try to blame somebody else, but apologise to anyone you have wronged. Ask God to forgive you and try, with his help, not to make the same mistake again.

(Excuses)

Wee Johnny's lazy eye

I want to tell you about the time wee Johnny had a lazy eye. How many of you know what that is? A lazy eye is an eye which doesn't work as hard or as quickly as the other eye and sometimes, because it is lazy, it develops a squint. The cure for a lazy eye seems very odd - it is to cover up the good eye and do nothing at all with the bad eye. The day Johnny got his good eye covered he couldn't understand it and he asked endless questions. His Mammy tried to explain that when one eye was covered, the other eye had to work twice as hard and, through time, by working harder on its own it becomes stronger and more active. It is what is called "The Law of Compensation'.

His Mammy said that when one eye is put out of action the other eye becomes stronger. In the same way, if one ear is put out of action the other ear is more active. "Do you understand now", she asked. "Perfectly", answered Johnny and winking with his lazy eye he said, "Did you ever notice that when a person has a short leg - the other one is always longer!"

Although Johnny was only joking he saw at once how the law of compensation worked and how it affected the lives of people in countless ways. You know there are millions and millions of people in the world and yet no two of them are exactly similar. We are all different and we all have different gifts. Some people are clever, others are not so clever. Some people are musical, others not so musical. Some people are naturally handy, other are clumsy. And so we could go on - but the point is that the law of compensation runs through the whole of life. When people are deprived of one talent, so another talent is more active. The really important thing is to make the best use of the talents we have, and to learn to never never look down on others who have different gifts from us.

(Gifts: Matthew ch. 25 vs. 14-30; Romans ch. 12 vs. 6-8)

The Collecting Box

One Sunday at Church there was a visiting minister and he was to have his lunch at wee Johnny's house. So Johnny was even more attentive than usual to all that happened during the service. After the benediction he waited for the minister to take him to his home. Just when they were leaving the church the sexton stopped them. In his hand he had a 50p piece and a great smile all over his face.

"This is for you", he said to the minister and then he explained. "You see", he said, "We have a box in the porch and anyone who is helped by the service is asked to put in a contribution for the minister. It has been there for a couple of years", he added, "and I look in it every Sunday but there has never been anything in it until today". So the minister took the 50p and thanked him and gave it to Johnny and they left the Church.

At lunch time Johnny could hardly contain himself. "See what I've got", he said to his Daddy and showed him the money. "Where did you get that?" asked his Daddy. Then the minister explained, "You know, there is a collecting box in the porch of your Church", he began. "Don't tell me", interrupted Johnny's Mammy, "that there was something in it today. Well, I'm delighted". "You see", said the minister, "when I came to the Church today, I was early and there was nobody about. When I saw the collecting box in the porch I thought it was for missions, or the hungry or some good cause so I put the 50p in it myself". Before anyone could speak wee Johnny exclaimed - "Wasn't it a pity you didn't put a pound in it". "Well maybe it is", said the minister, "but that box has taught me a lesson about life and the lesson is this - the more you put into it the more you get out of it". That's just what Jesus meant when he said "He that keepeth his life shall lose it - but he that loseth his life for my sake shall keep it unto life eternal".

(Commitment: John ch. 12 v. 25)

True greatness

One evening wee Johnny was out in the garden reading a book called "Great People of the World". There were stories about Alexander the Great; The Duke of Wellington; Lord Nelson; Scott of the Antarctic. When he finished reading he was watching the sun set in great clouds of red and gold and he felt a real longing in his heart to do something great and glorious. He wanted to be a famous man. He said to his sister, "Do you think it is wrong to wish to be great?" "I don't know", said his sister, "You better ask Daddy". So he ran into the house and said to his Daddy, "I want to be a great man. Is that wrong Daddy?"

"Not at all", said his Daddy, "I'm very glad you want to be great". "I want to be great and high above everybody else such as a field-marshal or an admiral", said Johnny. His Daddy shook his head. "If you think to be high up in the world is to be great, my boy, you're making a mistake". His Daddy pointed to the book case and explained that the books on the top shelf are not always the best books. "The best and most useful books are lower down, near at hand. The only way to be great is to be great in yourself, the secret is to learn to serve others".

"Oh", said Johnny, "If that's all, I can begin right away. Tell me what to do". "God will tell you what to do if you listen to His voice. Is there anything, even a small thing, that you ought to do now?" said his Daddy. "Well", said Johnny very slowly, "I should feed the rabbits because I forgot to feed them this morning". "Right", said his Daddy, "that's what God has been telling you to do". "Oh, but it's such a little thing", said Johnny, "I want Him to give me something hard".

"No", said his Daddy, "The little duty that lies in front of you is the great thing in God's sight. Only by doing the little duties well can you learn to be great".

(Greatness: Matthew ch. 20 vs. 20-28)

Johnny learning French

Wee Johnny has started to learn French at school and, all of a sudden, he has become very polite and a little bit conceited. Now when he wants anything he says, "please" not in English of course, but in French - "s'il vous plaît" - and when he gets something he says, "thanks" in French, "merci". And when he makes a mistake he says "sorry", not in English but in French - "pardonnez-moi". Everyone in the house soon got tired of Johnny's French - "merci", "pardonnez-moi", "s'il vous plaît". He was at it all the time and one day his sister said to him, "It's a pity, Johnny, you had to learn French before you had some manners". His Daddy said, "Well I suppose it's better to be polite in French than not to be polite at all". Do you know what his Mammy said? She said, "I hope Johnny when you are saying your prayers you will say your three French phrases to God, for these are the three things we should all say in our prayers.

Thank you, forgive me and please".

Will you remember them? Merci, pardonnez-moi and s'il vous plaît.

(Manners; Prayer)

FOR A
Wonderful
MUM

The blue beads

A few days before Mother's Day, wee Johnny opened his money box and took out all the money he had saved. He wanted to buy his Mammy something really special as a present for Mother's Day. He went to a shop in town where they sold jewellery. He looked in the window at the necklaces and brooches and then he saw a beautiful string of blue beads. He went into the shop and he asked the man if he could see the blue beads. He said, "I would like to buy them for my Mammy for Mother's Day; I want to give her a beautiful present". The shopkeeper knew that Johnny wouldn't have enough money to pay for them but he said nothing.

"I'll take them", said Johnny, "How much are they?" He put all the money he had down on the counter and the man parcelled them up and said, "I hope your Mammy likes them". His Mammy was delighted with the lovely blue beads and she gave Johnny a big kiss and thanked him very much. His Mammy wondered how Johnny could pay for the expensive beads so next day she went to the shop and asked the shopkeeper. He said, "Johnny paid the biggest price anyone could ever pay because he gave all that he had".

Boys and girls that is what Jesus did for love of us "He gave all He had". I hope you will never forget that and that you will try to show your gratitude to Him who has done so much for you.

(Mother's Day / Gratitude: Romans ch. 8 v. 32)

'Say thank you darling'

It was Children's Day in wee Johnny's Church and the Sunday School prizes were going to be given out.

This was the first time wee Johnny had got a prize at Church. He was very small and very shy but he hadn't missed a day at Sunday School and he was all excited. His Mammy was excited too. She dressed him very carefully and told him over and over again how to go up for his prize. He wasn't to hurry, not to run, he was to shake hands with the minister and, above all, he was to say "thank-you". There were lots of prizes and wee Johnny's was near the end. He listened very carefully to every name that was called and when at last he heard his own name he jumped up so excitedly and just as he was leaving the seat his Mammy whispered, "Don't forget to say 'Thank You' darling". Wee Johnny half walked and half ran up the aisle. He shook hands with the minister and when he got his prize he said in a big loud voice, "Thank you darling". Although it made everyone smile, it also made everyone think, for here was a little boy who had two great virtues - thankfulness and obedience.

So I hope you don't forget to be grateful, not just for your prize but for all the kind people who love you and help you. And remember always that the best way you can show your gratitude is by being obedient.

(Gratitude)

1066 A.D.

How many of the boys and girls know what a howler is? It is a mistake which makes us laugh. Most howlers are made by boys and girls usually in school. They are called howlers because they are supposed to make us howl with laughter. I remember once seeing a whole book of howlers and some of them were very funny. Let me tell you some of them.

Queen Victoria was the longest queen on the throne.

Solomon was the wisest man because he had so many wives to advise him.

Some cows are very dangerous, especially bulls.

Days are longer in Summer than in Winter because heat expands everything.

William the Conqueror landed in 1066 A.D. - A.D. means after dark.

I am sure you all know that Solomon was the wisest man not because he had so many wives, but because he asked God to give him wisdom. I am sure you all know that the days are longer in Summer because the earth goes round the sun once a year. It leans at an angle to the sun so that our part of the earth gets more of the sun in Summer. That is why the days are longer.

I am sure you all know that A.D. does not mean after dark. It means the very opposite - it comes from the Latin word - Anno Domini - which means the year of the Lord. So that 1066 A.D. mean 1066 years after the birth of Jesus. Certainly any year which is A.D. is not after dark, because Jesus said "I am the light of the world". He came into the world to destroy darkness, the darkness of sin. He did that by giving His life on the cross. When we love and serve Him we too become lights - lights to guide others to Jesus and to help to banish the darkness of sin from the world.

(Light: John ch. 8 v. 12)

Speaking the truth in love

On wee Johnny's last birthday his Aunt Mary gave him a nice white linen handkerchief. It's not the kind of present a wee boy would get excited about. A few days later he had to go with his Mammy to visit his Aunt and he didn't want to go. You see Aunt Mary lived in a house by herself and when Johnny went to visit her he had nothing to do but sit and listen to his Aunt and his Mammy talking. However he had to go and that was that. "Don't forget to thank Aunt Mary for your birthday present", said his Mammy as they came to the house. When they were inside, Johnny said to his Aunt, "Thank you very much for the nice handkerchief". "Sure it's not worth mentioning", replied his Aunt. "That's what I thought", said Johnny, "but Mammy said I was to thank you".

At that Johnny laughed, his Aunt smiled and his Mammy looked at him crossly. Soon they had tea which Johnny didn't like very much and then he had to sit and listen to his Aunt and Mammy talking and talking and talking. At last his Mammy stood up and said, "We'll have to go". "Well Johnny", said his Aunt when they were saying good-bye, "Did you enjoy your afternoon?"

"No, indeed I didn't", said Johnny bluntly. "Well, maybe you'll come again some other day", said his Aunt. "Not unless I have to", said Johnny.

That night at bed time Johnny got a lecture from his Mammy. "You know Johnny, you were very rude to your Aunt today". "Oh, I know that", said Johnny. "but I had to be rude". "What do you mean?" asked his Mammy. "Well you have told me I should always tell the truth and it's hard sometimes to tell the truth and not be rude". "I know it's not easy", said his Mammy, "but there are two texts from the Bible to help you. First, from the Old Testament,

"There is a time to speak and a time to keep silent". Second, from the New Testament, Paul writes, "Speaking the truth in love". "I think", said his Mammy, "if we remember these two verses they will help us to be truthful and, at the same time, be kind".

(Truth: Ecclesiastes ch. 3 v. 7; Ephesians ch. 4 v. 15)

Whose side are you on?

One day there was a football match between the Anchor Boys and the Cubs. Wee Johnny played for the Anchor Boys and like everything he did, he put his whole heart into it.

It was a very even match and at half time there was no score. After half time one of the Cubs got the ball and rushed down the field with it. Wee Johnny went after him but before he could tackle him, the Cubs had scored a goal. All the boys on the Cubs' side cheered but wee Johnny shouted "off-side". The referee pointed to the centre spot because it was a very good goal. But Johnny wasn't satisfied and he ran up to the referee and said, "He was off-side, Sir". "No, he wasn't off-side", the referee replied, "it was a good goal".

"Oh Sir", said Johnny, who was determined to have the last word, "whose side are you on?"

Well, of course a good referee should not be on one side or the other. But if wee Johnny was wrong about refereeing - he was right about life - for in life we have to be on one side or the other. This is very true when we are trying to follow Jesus. You just can't be neutral if you are a Christian. This is why Jesus said, "No man can serve two masters - and he that is not with me is against me". When it comes to religion you have to choose whose side you are on. So let me ask you wee Johnny's question - whose side are you on?

(Choice: Matthew ch. 6 v. 24; Luke ch. 11 v. 23)

Johnny's Prayer

One night when Johnny was getting ready for bed it was very cold and there was no heat in his bedroom, so his Mammy allowed him to undress and put on his pyjamas at the fire in the living room. His Mammy and his Granny were sitting at each side of the fire and Johnny took off his clothes and folded them into a neat bundle. Then he put on his pyjamas, his dressing gown and his slippers.

"I think Mammy", he said, "I'll just say my prayers here before I go to my room". "Very well", said his Mammy. So Johnny knelt down at her knees and began his prayers.

"God bless Mammy and Daddy and help me to be a good boy. Bless me at school. Make me more like Jesus". Then he raised his voice and he spoke very loudly, "Please God send me a new bicycle. Amen". "You know Johnny", said his Mammy, "there's no need to shout your prayers like that. God isn't deaf". "I know God isn't deaf", answered Johnny, "but Granny doesn't hear unless you shout".

You see, although Johnny was praying for a new bicycle, he thought God might send it to him through his Granny.

And of course God often answers our prayers like that. Many of his greatest gifts come to us through other people - a happy home, a good school, our books, our toys, our holidays. There are lots of things we get from those who love us and they are really gifts from God - for He is the giver of all. But when we ask God for anything we should leave it to Him to find the best way of answering our prayers.

We should never never forget to be thankful - not only for all God's gifts but also for the wonderful people He uses to send them to us.

(Gratitude)

L Plate: G.B.

Boys and girls you all know what this is and what it means. This is an L Plate and it means that the person who has it on his car is a learner. Like most wee boys Johnny is very keen on cars and he just can't wait until he is 17 and able to learn to drive. He won't be too hard to teach for he already knows what the pedals and all the knobs are for and how they work. One Saturday he was out on his bicycle with his friend and a car passed them. It was going slowly but didn't give them much room. "I bet that's a learner", said Johnny and, sure enough, when the car passed it had an L Plate on its back bumper and it was a lady driving. As well as the "L" it had another plate like this: - G.B. "Maybe it's a girl from the Girls' Brigade", said Johnny's friend. "Not at all", said Johnny, "It means that though she is still a learner she is getting better". We might learn from that a lesson about following Jesus. Everyone who follows Jesus is a disciple and the world disciple means simply "Learner". And if we are good disciples we will also be getting better every day.

But what else does L stand for? Well it stands for 50. It is the Roman number for 50. I am telling you this because, 50 years ago, there was a little boy started Sunday School for the first time and he is in Church to-day. He started Sunday School here in Trinity and he has missed very few Sundays in 50 years. His name is Mr. Monteith. He started as a boy, then he became a teacher and now he is Superintendent. 50 years at Sunday School. Isn't that a great record. So on behalf of all the boys and girls past and present I say "Thank you Mr. Monteith and many happy returns".

(Disciple; 50th Anniversary: Matthew ch. 11 v. 29)

Johnny at the Zoo

One day wee Johnny and his Daddy went to Belfast by bus. Johnny's Daddy got all his business finished early so he suggested they would visit the Zoo. They got a bus out to the Zoo and it was a great experience for Johnny, as he had often seen pictures of wild animals but he had never seen them alive. When they arrived they walked round and Johnny was tremendously interested.

What he liked best of all was the lions. He would have stood and watched them all day and he kept on asking questions. Where did they come form? What did they eat? Were they really as fierce as people believed? His Daddy did his best to answer everything and he finished by telling the story of a lion that escaped from a circus and killed several people before it was captured. Johnny listened thoughtfully and then he said, "If the lion in this cage happened to get out and eat you Daddy, what bus would I take to get home?"

At first it seems a very silly and selfish question. You see what Johnny wanted to do was to be ready for every emergency. He took to himself the boy scout motto "Be Prepared".

That, boys and girls, is a very important thing in life. The great secret of being ready for anything is to learn not to put your trust in things which are uncertain but to depend on the God who never changes. Live in the friendship and fellowship of Jesus and you will be like the wise man in the parable of Jesus who built his house on the rock and the rain descended and the floods came and the winds blew and beat upon that house and it fell not for it was founded on a rock.

(Be prepared: Matthew ch. 6 vs. 19, 20 and ch. 7 vs. 24-27)

Pickpocket and the Bible

How many of the boys and girls have got nicknames? Some people get nicknames because of the way they look - like Lofty or Ginger, or because of their name like Mac or Pinkie or because of the way they behave like Grumpy or Smiler. I want to tell you a true story about a man who was nicknamed "Pickpocket". Do you know what a pickpocket is? He is a special kind of thief - a thief who picks pockets, or who takes things from peoples' pockets. He was a pickpocket in New York and he had just been released from prison. He was walking down a busy crowded street and the old temptation came to him. He picked a pocket and he thought he had got a big fat wallet. He went to the park where it was quiet, to see what he had got and to his surprise it was a leather-bound Bible. He opened it at the Sermon on the Mount and read what Jesus said. He decided to live a new life and he asked for God's forgiveness and prayed for strength to stand against temptation.

God heard him and answered his prayer and he became an honest man and spent the rest of his life helping others and serving God. This all happened through reading the Bible. The best book to read is the Bible.

(The Bible: John ch. 17 v. 17)

Johnny's breakfast

One time wee Johnny was staying for a holiday with his aunt and he was having a great time. The first morning he was there his Auntie had grapefruit for breakfast. When Johnny tasted it he found it was bitter and said, "I don't like grapefruit".

The next morning when he came down for breakfast he found a plate of cornflakes. "I never take cornflakes", he said to his Aunt. "Well Johnny", said his Aunt, "you don't like grapefruit and you don't take cornflakes - tell me what does you Mammy make at home?". "She makes porridge", said Johnny and that settled it. Next morning there was porridge for breakfast. But when Johnny came to the table he just sat and looked at his plate. "Eat up", said his Aunt. "I never eat porridge", said Johnny."What do you mean Johnny?" said his Aunt, crossly. "You told me yesterday that your Mammy always makes porridge at home". "That's right", said Johnny, "but I never take it".

I don't know what you would say to a boy like that. But I do know that he wasn't very grateful for all that was being done to try to please him. I wonder if any of you boys and girls are like that. I hope that doesn't happen in your house. Never forget, boys and girls, how much is being done for you at home by those who love you.

Once Jesus healed ten lepers and only one of them came back to give thanks. We don't think much of the other nine because nobody likes to see a person who is ungrateful.

To give thanks is simply good manners - but as well as that it is what the Bible teaches.

The Psalms tell us to come to God with thanksgiving. Paul often tells the people - to give thanks.

(Gratitude: Psalm 100 v. 4; Luke ch. 17 vs. 11-19)

Kindness to animals

One day in school the teacher was giving a lesson on kindness to animals. Before she finished she asked a question to drive the lesson home and to make sure everyone had taken it in. "If I was going along the road and a donkey and cart came along with a heavy load and I began to push the cart to help the donkey along, what virtue would I be practising?" Up shot wee Johnny's hand. "Well Johnny", said the teacher, "what virtue?" "Please miss, brotherly love".

Of course it was only one of Johnny's jokes, but it wasn't so far from the truth. If the dumb animals are not our brothers they are our friends and very good friends too. How much we owe to them. They work for us and they bring us a wealth of friendship and companionship. They provide us with much of our food and some of our clothes. This is Animals' Welfare Week and I have been asked to deliver a message from those who cannot speak for themselves. "Because children can be our best friends we want you to think of us this week. What we need is very much what you need - food and drink; warmth and shelter; freedom to run about and play; friendship and sympathy. Often we don't get these things".

This message comes to you today from the animals, the dumb creatures which God has made to help us and be our friends. I hope that you will always be kind to them.

SAVE THE WHALE
USPCA
SPECIES
THE RAINFOREST

How much you live

One Saturday night wee Johnny was learning his Sunday School lessons. He always knew his lessons very well.

He had question 15 in his Catechism - "Who was the oldest man in the world?" But when he looked at the answer he couldn't pronounce it - Methuselah. He asked his Mammy how to pronounce it and then he repeated it over and over again to try to remember. When he began to think about it - 969 years old, he couldn't believe it. Then his Mammy got him to read about it in Genesis chapter 5. Then suddenly Johnny asked his Mammy, "If I happened to live longer than Methuselah, would they take his name out and put mine in?" His Mammy said none of us would live to the age of 969, but what does it matter anyway.

God doesn't count a person's life by the number of years he lives but by the service he puts into it. Jesus was only 33 years of age when he died on the cross, and yet he lived more fully and did more than the oldest man in the world. And so you see the important thing is not how long you live but how much you live. Not the length of your life but the quality of your life. If you want to really live you will give yourself to the service of God and follow in the footsteps of Jesus.

(Service; Methuselah: Matthew ch. 20 vs. 20-28)

Boys will be boys

One day Johnny's Mammy was having a visitor to tea and she had warned Johnny to be good when he came in from school. It was just one of those days - Johnny was really a nuisance to everyone. He was noisy, he was untidy and then he ate some of the sandwiches his Mammy had prepared for the tea. His Mammy was cross and she scolded him and told him to go to his room. "Don't be too hard on him", said the visitor, "Boys will be boys".

This expression is used sometimes as an excuse when a boy has done something he ought not to have done. It just means there is nothing to be surprised about when a boy forgets himself and oversteps the mark and does something out of place. We expect boys to do that sometimes. I once heard of a boys' school and the motto was "Boys will be men".

It is very important that older people should remember that the boys of today are the men of tomorrow. It is also important for the boys to remember it themselves. When you are young you are laying the foundation of your whole life and what you build later depends on the foundation you are laying now. Learn then to take advantage of every opportunity and to appreciate everything that is being done to help you.

Above all learn when you are young to give God the first place in your heart for that is the best foundation of all.

(Boys: Matthew ch. 6 v. 33)

Nick-names

Boys and girls I want to talk to you about names. Some of you have only got one Christian name, some two and some have three. I wonder is there any boy or girl in Church with more than three Christian names. Some Royal babies have got four Christian names. (Princess Anne is called Victoria Anne Mary Elizabeth, such a lot of names for a tiny baby). Of course a whole lot of us have got extra names, names our parents never gave us. We often get them when we go to school. We call them nicknames.

Now a nickname means just, plain and simply, an extra name. Sometimes we give people nicknames because of how they look. A person with red hair we call Ginger or Carrots. A tall person is called Lanky or Lofty. A small person is called Tich. There are all sorts of names like that. Sometimes we give nicknames because of what a person's nature is like. A cross person is Grumpy. A happy person is Smiler.

Then there are some famous nicknames. Ethelred - The Unready; Richard - The Lionheart; William - The Conqueror. The Bible has some nicknames Abraham, The Friend of God; Solomon - The Wise; Job - The Patient. There was one man in the Bible whose name was changed by Jesus because his whole nature was transformed. He was one of the first disciples. When Jesus met him he was called Simon - Simon meant sand. But when his life was changed Jesus called him Peter and Peter means rock. You see Simon was unsteady, uncertain and undependable - just like the sand. But after he let Jesus into his heart he became strong, sure and steady as a rock. Boys and girls, Jesus can do that for us. He can change us from grumpy to happy, from gloomy to glad and He will do it for us if we let Him into our hearts.

(Conversion)

Thank you

Boys and girls I want to read you a letter which I cut out from the Belfast Telegraph. This letter is from a little girl guide. It is headed "Thank You Mr. Baxter"

'Sir,
On my way home from the Girl Guides on Thursday last I lost my tenderfoot card. It was returned to me by first post on Saturday morning by a Mr. Baxter, but he did not enclose his address. I just want to thank him for his thoughtful act.

Yours,
Carole E. Wilson (Age 10)
12 Florence Place, Belfast'.

Isn't that a lovely letter. It shows us the virtue of kindness and consideration on the part of Mr. Baxter and it shows us the virtue of gratitude on the part of Carole Wilson (Age 10).

I wonder what you would have done if you had been Mr. Baxter? Would you have gone to the trouble of getting an envelope and a stamp and posting the lost card? I do hope that's what you would all have done, for that is the spirit of Jesus.

I wonder what you would have done if you had been Carole Wilson? Would you have gone to the trouble of writing a letter to the paper to say thank you? I hope you would for, again, that is the spirit of Jesus. The girls may not be guides and the boys may not be scouts and you may never lose your tenderfoot card but, believe me, you have plenty of opportunities to show kindness to others and even more to be grateful for kindness to yourself.

There are two great virtues which every follower of Jesus should be careful to put into practice - kindness to others and thankfulness to others.

(Kindness: Ephesians ch. 4 v. 32)

The road to royalty

How would you answer if I asked you who is the first King mentioned in the Bible. I must tell you it's a trick question because the answer is King James I, King of Great Britain, France and Ireland. Why is this? Well, it was at the command of King James that the Bible was translated into English and at the beginning of every Bible there is a printed address written to the King by the men who translated the Bible.

But the first Biblical King is King Saul and do you know how he became King. Saul's father was a rich man with much land and many animals. One day he lost a herd of donkeys so he sent for his son Saul and said to him, "Take one of the servants and go and look for the donkeys". Saul had to travel a great distance seeking the herd of donkeys and while looking for them he met the prophet Samuel. Samuel had a message from God telling him to anoint Saul as King. And so Saul, doing a very simple and humble duty, found the way to greatness.

I would like to tell you a story about an advertisement which appeared in a Chicago newspaper offering a reward of 5,000 dollars for the arrest of a person who murdered a policeman some years before. A reporter wondered about this and discovered that, 12 years ago, a young man was found guilty and was in prison. But why was the case reopened and who was offering the reward? He found out that the reward was offered by an old lady living in a poor part of the city. She was the mother of the boy in prison. She knew her son was innocent and so she had scrubbed floors and saved every penny for 12 years. The newspaper took up the case and the mother's faith was justified by the release of her son. This was a great day for the mother, a great achievement - how? By scrubbing floors. Just an ordinary every day task.

That was how Saul found his kingdom and came to greatness. And it's still the same. Only when we are faithful and true in ordinary little things does God call us to greater service.

(Faithfulness: Luke ch. 16 v. 10)

Johnny's fountain pen

One time wee Johnny was doing an Examination at school and his Daddy promised to buy him a fountain pen if he passed. And you can be sure Johnny made no mistakes. The day he got the results his Daddy took him down the town to buy the pen. As they came near the shop Johnny noticed a great big pen, as big as himself, hanging at the door. "That's the pen I want", he announced. "But you can't have that", said his Daddy, "That's not a real pen, it's only an advertisement and even if you could hold it, you couldn't write with it". "Why not?" asked Johnny. "Because I tell you it's only an advertisement". So they went into the shop and Johnny picked a beautiful pen. He filled it with ink and wrote his name with it and his Daddy bought it. It was a very happy little boy that went to bed that night and his last thought was about his new pen.

It's not surprising that Johnny had a dream. He dreamt he was in Church, but it wasn't an ordinary Church. Instead of people in the pews there were fountain pens; and instead of a minister in the pulpit - what do you think there was? There was a fountain pen; not an ordinary one like those in the pews; no indeed. But a great big one just like the one outside the shop that Johnny wanted his Daddy to buy. And the big pen was preaching a sermon; this was what it was saying, "If you want to be a good fountain pen, there are three conditions you must fulfil. First, you must be filled. Second, you must be kept clean and third, you must be guided by a good hand". The next morning at breakfast Johnny told his dream. "Well", said his Daddy, "that is true not only for fountain pens but also for people and it is true in particular for boys and girls. If you want to be good, there are three conditions you must fulfil. You must be filled, filled with the Spirit of Christ. You must be kept clean, clean in thought and word and deed. And you must be guided by a good hand - the hand of God".

(Johnny's fountain pen: Ephesians ch. 5 v. 18; 1 Timothy ch. 5 v. 22b; 1 Peter ch. 5 v. 6; James ch. 3 v. 17)

You're a brick

"You're a brick", was an expression that wee Johnny's Mammy used quite often. When wee Johnny fell and hurt himself his Mammy would give him a big hug and say, "Don't cry Johnny, you're a brick". Or perhaps when Johnny was taking some horrible medicine without making a fuss, she would say, "You're a brick Johnny".

It's such a funny expression. It sounds so silly calling a person "A brick". I wonder how many of the boys and girls know the story behind it.

Long ago in the days of Ancient Greece, one of the most famous cities was called Sparta. One day a visitor remarked to the King of Sparta how strange it was that such an important city had no walls to defend it.

The King pointed to his soldiers and said, "There are the walls of Sparta, ten thousand men and every man a brick". Every man was prepared to fight for Sparta, to guard the city with his life, every man was a brick in its unseen wall of defence. So when anyone is brave or unselfish we say "You're a brick".

Bricks are made for building and boys and girls can be used to build the City of God, the city of love and peace. Every time you are hurt or disappointed but are brave and smile; every time you are tempted to lose your temper but hold it back and are gentle instead; every time you want something yourself but give it up for someone else, you are building a brick into the unseen walls of the great and glorious City of God.

*(Living stones:
1 Peter
ch. 2 vs. 4, 5)*

Wee Johnny's dog

Boys and girls I want to tell you about wee Johnny's dog. His names was Sport. He and Johnny were great friends and they had endless fun together. Wherever Johnny was, you were almost sure to find Sport. One Sunday when Johnny and his Daddy were going to Church, Sport slipped out of the house and followed them. They didn't notice him until they reached the Church door. It was too late to take him home again so they wondered what they should do. They decided to go into the back seat and let Sport lie under the pew. He was allowed to stay there on one condition - he had to lie perfectly still all through the service. This happened almost every Sunday and Johnny's Daddy said, "If Sport makes any noise or disturbs anyone in the congregation he will never come to Church again". Everything was all right until one Sunday there was a very long sermon and Johnny started swinging his legs back and forwards from the edge of his seat. And then it happened. His heel went back too far and hit poor Sport on the head and the dog gave a loud yelp.

Next Sunday his Daddy made sure Sport was left behind. Although wee Johnny pleaded and said it was all his fault, Sport was closed in the kitchen when they went to Church. As soon as they had gone Sport began to try to get out. He tried the door, but it was firmly closed and then he tried the window. It was open a very little bit at the bottom, but it was enough to let him get his nose in. Little by little he worked until he got his head out and it wasn't long until he was all out. Sport ran along the road wagging his tail and in the middle of the second singing he pushed into the pew and lay down. I needn't tell you what Johnny and his Daddy talked about on the way home from Church.

"Isn't he a great wee dog", said Johnny, "and so clever". "Why do you think he did that?" asked his Daddy. "Well", said Johnny, "there were two reasons - first, because he was in the habit of going to Church on Sunday and second, because he knew that his master would be there".

"That's right", said his Daddy, "He's a clever dog indeed, for that's why we go to Church ourselves - because, like Jesus, it is our custom to go and because we know that our Master is there".

Wouldn't it be a good thing if we would all follow the example of Jesus and make it our custom to come to Church on Sunday. But, if you have dog, take my advice and leave it at home and make sure that all the doors and windows are firmly closed.

(Church going)

The good deed

One day at the 'Cubs', the Cub mistress was reminding the boys of their duty to do a good deed every day. She went over all the boys and asked them to tell her what good deed they had done that day. Some of them had helped in the house, others had worked in the garden and some of them had run messages. There was a great variety of good deeds the boys had done. Then it was wee Johnny's turn to answer. "Well Johnny", said the Cub mistress, "what good deed did you do today?" "Please Miss", said Johnny, "Jimmy and I helped an old lady across the road". "Well now, that's very good", said the Cub mistress, "but why did it take the two of you to do that?" "Well, you see", answered wee Johnny, "she didn't want to go across the road".

It wasn't much of a good deed that. Of course it's a good thing to do a good turn every day. You will always find plenty of opportunities to do something really helpful. There are lots of things to be done and there are lots of people who need your help and who will be very glad to get your help. If you do good deeds like that you will be following the example of Jesus who went about always and everywhere doing good.

(Doing good; Matthew ch. 7 v. 12; Ephesians ch. 2 v. 10)

Road to my Aunty Jean's

One day in the summer wee Johnny had gone on his bicycle to visit his Aunty Jean. He had a lovely time as he liked helping on the farm. On his way home when he came to the fork on the road, a car came along and stopped beside Johnny. The man in the car put down his window and pointing to one road he said to Johnny, "Where does this road go?" "I don't know", said Johnny. "Well", said the driver, "do you know where the other road goes?" "Oh yes", said Johnny, "It goes to my Aunty Jean's".

It wasn't quite as simple an answer as you might think because Johnny knew what was important in his own little world and he was sure about that.

It's good on the road of life to know where you are going. A good plan is to carry a map and learn to read it. There is a map for the journey of life and it is the Bible. It is given to guide our feet in the right paths and if we follow its guidance we will take very few wrong turns. It is a great thing to be young to be starting life's journey. Before you there lies a whole world of new experience and new discovery. Make sure you make the best of it. Take the advice of those who are older who have travelled the road before and, above all, let Jesus be your guide. If you come to a fork and you don't know which road to take, ask Jesus and He will direct you for He is your Guide, your Counsellor and your Friend.

(Guidance: Psalm 48 v. 14)

STAMPS
13p
POST OFFICE
RULES

Wrong change

One Saturday morning Johnny had nothing to do and he was just sitting about the house. His Mammy asked him to do a message. She said, "I have some letters to write and I have no stamps, would you please go to the Post Office and get me six 13p stamps?" She gave him £1 and told him he could keep the change. Johnny wasn't long working out what he would have for himself - 22p.

Johnny got out his bicycle and cycled to the Post Office. It was very busy and Johnny had to wait his turn. Eventually his turn came and he asked for six 13p stamps and gave the lady £1. The lady gave him his stamps and his change and he turned away. As he walked to the door and looked at his change he thought there was a mistake. He counted it again - yes it was wrong.

He went back to the counter and said to the lady, "You have given me the wrong change". The lady never looked at the money but said sharply, "You should have told me before you left the counter - you can't have your change corrected. That's the rule of the Post Office". "Well", said Johnny, "If that's the rule I suppose you have to stick to it, but I just wanted to say you gave me 10p too much".

From Johnny learn the lesson of simple honesty and not to take advantage of another person's mistake. From the lady in the Post Office learn not to jump to conclusions and always be ready to think the best and not the worst of others.

(Honesty)

Changing one sock

One Sunday wee Johnny was up early and was washed and dressed and had his breakfast. He had his hymn book and Bible collected and was just setting off for Sunday School when his Mammy noticed he had a hole in his sock. "Run upstairs", said his Mammy, "and change that sock". He was up, had changed and was down before you could say 'Jack Robinson' and with a great rush he set off for Sunday School. When he came home and had his dinner he was sitting at the fire and his Mammy noticed something peculiar. Johnny had on two different socks! They were both grey but one was plain and the other one fancy. "Look at your socks", said his Mammy, "They don't match". "I know", said Johnny, "but I did what you said. I changed that sock". Johnny had only changed the sock with the hole and then the two socks didn't match.

Now, boys and girls, of course it's a good thing to be obedient and to do what you are told but it's even better to do more than you are told. I wonder if any of you know a text from the Bible which tells us to do that. Here it is in the words of Jesus, "Whosoever shall compel thee to go a mile, go with him twain". That means that if we want to be like Jesus we must not stop with what we are told to do or what we are expected to do. We should always do more. I hope you will remember that and the next time you are told to run and change a sock, make sure to change both of them. Always be ready to do more than you are asked. That's what we call going the second mile and it fulfils the command of Jesus - "Whosoever shall compel you to go a mile, go with him twain".

(Second mile: Matthew ch. 5 v. 41)

Encouragement

When wee Johnny was on holidays this year at Portrush his older sister Mary and her boyfriend were there too. His name was Peter and Johnny and Peter got on very well together.

You see Peter had plenty of money so he had a lovely car, a power boat and water skis. He often took Johnny out in his car and his boat and he started to teach him to water ski. As well as that, he was very generous and bought Johnny lots of sweets and ice cream. Near the end of the holiday Peter had a birthday and Mary wanted to give him a nice present. It was a bit of a problem to know what to give him because he had everything. She decided to ask her mother. "Mum, what should I give him?" "I don't know", said her mother. "I know", said Johnny, "Give him plenty of encouragement".

Plenty of encouragement - that's what we all need no matter what else we may have. It is something that doesn't cost much to those who give it and yet it is priceless to those who receive it. So what about giving a bit of encouragement to your Mummy and Daddy. You know how much they do for you. Well you can encourage them by being obedient and unselfish. What about giving a bit of encouragement to your teacher in school? You can do that by always being early, helpful and attentive.

What about giving a bit of encouragement to your Church? You can do that by coming regularly to the service and to Sunday School. You can encourage your Sunday School teacher by learning your lessons and listening quietly. You can encourage your minister by your attendance and by being reverent in Church.

So remember: Give plenty of encouragement

(Encouragement)

Sore tummy - sore head

On Saturday morning wee Johnny asked his Mammy to have the tea early because there were a number of things he wanted to see on T.V. There was American Football, 'Jim'll Fix It' and a good western.

But Johnny's Mammy went into town to shop and she didn't get home until almost 5 o'clock. For once Johnny helped her to set the table and did everything he could to hurry things on but, for all that, he had only a few moments to gobble up his tea. "Take you time", said his Mammy, "and eat your tea properly". But Johnny only ate one piece of bread and half a cup of tea and away he rushed to the T.V. As soon as the western was over Johnny got up and said, "I think I'll go to bed". "What's wrong?"asked his Mammy. "I've got a pain in my tummy". said Johnny.

"Well, you know why", said his Mammy, "You didn't take your tea properly and your tummy's empty - there's nothing in it". However a glass of milk and a biscuit cured Johnny's pain and he went off to bed in good form.

Next morning Johnny was up early and dressed for church. They were all having breakfast together, but his Daddy wasn't in his usual good form. "What's wrong Daddy?" asked Johnny. "I didn't sleep too well, and I have a pain in my head". "Ah", said Johnny, "It's not because you didn't sleep well that you have a pain in your head. It's like my tummy - there's nothing in it". Johnny's Daddy laughed so heartily that his headache disappeared and they all set off for church.

It's a bad thing to have nothing in your tummy and it's worse to have nothing in your head, but there's something worse than both - it is to have nothing in your heart. If you have nothing in your heart, life is a vain and empty thing. But the wonderful thing is, if we ask Jesus He will come into our heart and give us a purpose to live for. That purpose is set out in the great commandment of Jesus - "Thou shalt love the Lord thy God with all thy heart and thy neighbour as thyself".

(Purpose: Matthew ch. 22 vs. 34-40)

Ladies first

One day in wee Johnny's class at school the teacher was giving a lesson on grammar. She had written on the blackboard a long list of sentences and in every one of them there was a mistake. There was a sentence for everybody in the class and each one in turn had to spot the mistake and then read out the sentence as it ought to be. Let me tell you some of them and see if you can find the mistakes. "It was the strangest sight I have ever saw". "Don't blame me, it was John who done it". "Please teacher, can I have the lend of your pencil". And so the sentences went on. Most of the boys and girls saw the mistakes at once and were able to correct them. But wee Johnny, for once, was not as clever as he thought. His sentence was a very easy one. "The horse and the cow is in the field". I'm sure you all know that it should be "The horse and the cow are in the field".

But wee Johnny didn't think of that. "Please teacher", he said, "it should be 'The cow and the horse is in the field'". "Why do you think that?" asked the teacher. "Well", said Johnny, "it should always be ladies first".

You know wee Johnny wasn't so far wrong after all. For if he didn't know good grammar, at least he knew good manners.

That's a far more important thing. It's nice to hear a person speaking correctly but it's far better to see a person acting correctly. And so boys and girls, or should I say girls and boys, always be careful of your speech but be even more careful of your actions for deeds count more than words with God.

(Manners)

Thank you for harvest baskets

Boys and girls I want to say 'thank you' to you today for all the lovely harvest baskets you brought to Church last Sunday. They were filled with such delicious things, all kinds of fruit, sweets and nuts.

During the week we delivered many of them to the sick and older members of our congregation and the rest were brought to the Children's Ward in the hospital. I can tell you that your gifts brought great joy to many people. I want to thank you today and to remind you that the Bible tells us "It is a good thing to give thanks". I hope you will remember that and always try to be grateful.

Wee Johnny was going to a party once and his Mammy said to him, "Don't forget to say thank you when you are leaving". It was a good party and when he got home he was telling his Mammy all about it.

"I hope you said thanks", said his Mammy.

"I didn't say thank you", confessed Johnny.

"Why not?" asked his Mammy crossly.

"Well", said Johnny, "when we were coming away and saying goodbye the boy in front of me said thank you and the lady said 'Don't mention it'".

No matter what anybody says I want to thank you today and I hope, boys and girls, you will always remember that it is a good thing to give thanks.

(Gratitude: Psalm 106 v. 1)

Nitro-Chalk

Johnny and his Daddy were out driving one day and not many miles from Omagh, at a corner on the road, there was a very interesting advertisement.

Just at this particular place there is a steep hill on the field at the corner, and you can see the field plainly from the road. As you get closer you notice that there are some letters written in the grass and then you can make out very distinctly, 'Nitro Chalk'. "Oh stop", said Johnny, "I want to see this advertisement". "We can't stop on this corner", said his Daddy, "but we'll turn and drive past it again". His Daddy explained that Nitrochalk was a fertiliser and that this field had been marked out with the letters and then the fertiliser had been sown on each letter. The result was plain for everyone to see. Each letter stood out in fresh green grass and it was a most effective way to show the difference that Nitro-Chalk made. "I think that's a great advertisement", said Johnny, "You can really see it for yourself".

And so boys and girls it is the same with the message of Easter. It is good to read that God has raised up Jesus and that He is alive for evermore but it is a thousand times better to have the living proof within yourself. We can have that by opening our hearts and asking Him to come and live in us. Then we can give the world the proof that Jesus is living, not only by our words, but by living in the spirit of Jesus. That is the most effective advertisement of all for the kingdom of God.

You remember the words of Jesus - "By their fruits ye shall know them. By this shall all men know that ye are my disciples - that ye love one another".

(Easter: Matthew ch. 7 v. 16; John ch. 13 v. 35)

God's advert

Boys and girls, I hope you all had a good holiday. I have been talking to some of you and I have heard about the exciting holidays you have had. Where do you think wee Johnny went? Wee Johnny went to London and what a thrill that was for him. A whole week with his Daddy in London. Wasn't he a lucky boy! London is a wonderful place with so many interesting things to see and wee Johnny and his Daddy saw a lot of them. They visited Westminster Abbey, the Tower of London and St. Paul's. They also went to Buckingham Palace, the Houses of Parliament and the Horse Guards Parade. Johnny loved the crowds, the traffic and, above all, the tubes.

One night, as a special treat, he was allowed to stay up late to see the wonderful advertisements in Piccadilly Square. What a marvellous sight it was. Johnny just stood on the pavement in amazement, fascinated by the display of coloured lights flashing in and out, advertising all kinds of different things. He had never seen anything like it before and his Daddy could hardly persuade him to leave. On the way back to the hotel on the bus they passed a Church which was lit up inside and you could see the stained glass windows with all their different figures and colours. "O look", said Johnny, "even God has His advertisements".

That is very true. There are many things in the world which tell about God, things which reveal His beauty and His love. You can be an advertisement for God. For when we live to His glory and follow the example of Jesus we are showing the world what God is like. Perhaps it was something like this that Jesus had in mind when he said to His disciples long ago - "Let your light shine before men that they may see your good deeds and praise your father in heaven".

(Witness: Matthew ch. 5 v. 16)

DEFG
LMNO
RSTU
WXYZ
ALPHABET
MATHS
4+2=7
Teacher
Johnny Rules ok!

New boy at school

Wee Johnny was off school for two weeks because he had very bad 'flu and when he went back to school there was a new boy in his class. Although he had never seen the new boy before he had heard a lot about him from his school friends who visited him when he was sick.

"He's a great talker", they told him, "and he has a great opinion of himself". "Is he any good at football?" Johnny asked. "Not much", he was told, "He's too selfish, he never passes the ball". "That's bad", said Johnny, "If you want your team to win you mustn't keep the ball to yourself". There and then the new boy sank very low in Johnny's estimation. When Johnny went back to school he got a chance to talk to the new boy on his own. They were left in the class room alone and they got chatting. The new boy said, "I don't think much of this school. It's not nearly as nice as the school I went to before". Then he started boasting about his old school. He said that the teachers and the boys and everything was far better. "I was the head boy of my class", he said proudly, "and I was the best footballer and the best cricketer at the school". Then Johnny said, "Did anyone at your old school ever tell you that you were wonderful?" "Well no", said the new boy. "Well", said Johnny, "wherever did you get the idea?"

Well I needn't tell you, that was the end of the conversation. But it put an end to the new boy's boasting and he became a much nicer and more likeable boy.

We can learn a lesson in humility from this story. Nobody likes a person who is proud. Jesus hated pride.

Jesus told the story of the Pharisee and the Publican going into the Temple to pray and he finished the story with the words: "Everyone that exalteth himself shall be humbled and he that humbleth himself shall be exalted".

(Pride: Luke ch. 18 vs. 9-14; Proverbs ch. 16 v. 18)

The pig and the chicken

Boys and girls, this is the story of the pig and chicken. One day a pig and a chicken were walking down the street when they came to a hoarding with advertisements on it. There were all kinds of advertisements for many different things, and most of them were illustrated with pictures. In the middle of the hoarding there was a big picture. What do you think it was?

It was a plate with bacon and eggs on it. "Look", said the chicken, "isn't it nice to see our produce advertised". The pig thought for a moment before he replied and this is what he said. "It is all right for you", he said, "but when it comes to bacon and eggs, remember your share is only a contribution but mine is a sacrifice".

You see the difference. The chicken could supply the eggs and go on living but in order to supply the bacon the pig had to give its life.

There are many ways in which we can all take that story to ourselves for we are all called to contribute something of our time and talents and substance for the work of the Kingdom of God. And when it comes to giving do we make a sacrifice or merely give a contribution? There is a big difference. To give to God what costs us nothing is unworthy of the God who gave His only son, and it is far from the spirit of Jesus who gave Himself for us. We should never forget it.

(Giving: 2 Samuel ch. 24 v. 24)

Donkey in the garage

One night wee Johnny was out with his Daddy in the car. It was a cold, snowy and windy night and they were late when they came home. As they came into the driveway Johnny saw something in the garage by the headlights of the car.

When they came up to the garage Johnny saw that it was a donkey. A stray donkey had gone into the garage for shelter. Johnny and his Daddy had a discussion about what they should do. Johnny said, "Poor Neddy, you couldn't put him out a night like that. Sure there is anti-freeze in the car, and it will do the car no harm to sit out". And so Neddy was left in the garage and the car was left out. Next morning Johnny got up early and rushed out to the garage but the rain had stopped and Neddy was away.

The next night Johnny and his Daddy were out again and when they came back - guess what was there? Not a donkey but two donkeys. During the day Neddy had told one of his friends about the kind people who had let him stay in the shelter of their garage. So Neddy had brought his friend to share his nice, warm, new home.

Boys and girls there are two lessons we can learn from this story. Firstly, kindness to animals and secondly to share our blessings with others.

I hope you will put both into practice. We should be especially kind to animals in snow and frost, and we should remember always to be grateful for all the blessings God has given us and share with others less fortunate than ourselves.

(Kindness; Sharing: Matthew ch. 5 v. 42)

Wheat and tares - which?

Boys and girls this is an important day in our congregation for as well as being full attendance day, it is Trinity Sunday. But it is also another day. It is Father's Day. I wonder if any of you bought a present for your Daddy. You know, it's not too late yet, because if you give your father your love and obedience for the rest of the day that's far better than any present you could buy in a shop.

Now it wouldn't do to have an important day like this without wee Johnny. One Sunday, the lesson in Sunday School was the parable of the wheat and the tares. The teacher explained how the farmer sowed good seed in his field but his enemies came by at night and sowed tares or weeds. The farmer decided to let both grow together until the harvest. Then they could both be reaped and the wheat separated from the tares. The teacher went on to explain that the parable was told to paint a picture of two kinds of people in the world - the good and the bad. She finished by asking the class which they would rather be - wheat or tares. Without much thought they all said they would rather be wheat - all but wee Johnny.

"I would rather be like the tares", he said. "But why?" asked the teacher. "Well", said Johnny, "the wheat may be good and the tares may be bad, but it was the wheat that got thrashed".

There may be some truth in Johnny's point of view but in the end it was the tares that were destroyed.

Now what is the lesson we can learn from this story? It is that while goodness sometimes brings hardship, in the end evil always bring destruction. Don't forget it, for it is very true in life.

(Wheat and tares; Father's Day: Matthew ch. 13 vs. 24-30)

The house with the golden windows

Wee Johnny was fascinated by a house away across the valley on the other side of the river. In the summer, when he was going to bed, he looked out his window and there, shining brightly, was the house with the most beautiful golden windows. Then in the morning when he looked out, the golden windows had disappeared. Johnny wondered about these windows and he kept wishing that there were golden windows in his house. One day Johnny's Daddy said that he would take him to see the house on the other side of the river. They had to drive about three miles to the bridge across the river. When Johnny arrived at the house there was a little boy just about his own age. "Please tell me the secret of your golden windows?" said Johnny. "Oh you've made a mistake", said the boy, "the house with the golden windows is on the other side of the river. Look over there".

Then Johnny realised that it was the sun that made all the difference. Johnny said, "In the morning it shines on our windows and makes them golden to you and in the evening it shines on this house and I look over at your golden windows".

When Johnny came home again he kept saying, "Our house has got golden windows". Boys and girls there is a lesson to learn from this story and that is to be content with the things around us and thankful for all the blessings we have. Remember the verse we read in the Bible "A fool's eyes wander to the ends of the earth".

(Contentment: Proverbs ch 17 v. 24)

Johnny's bus fare

One afternoon wee Johnny was invited to spend the afternoon with one of his friends from school. It wasn't far from the school, so they walked home when school was over but it would be dark when Johnny was coming home, so he was to come on the bus. It would only cost 10p but his Mammy gave him a 20p piece and told him not to lose it. Johnny and his friend had a great time together and after teatime wee Johnny had to go for the bus. When wee Johnny was seated on the bus he put his hand in his pocket but there was no 20p piece. He searched all his pockets, but he couldn't find it. What was he to do? Before long Johnny was in tears. When the conductor came to him he was still crying. The conductor said, "What's wrong with you?" Johnny explained he had lost his money. "Well", said the conductor, "I'll give you a ticket and pay for it myself". But that didn't stop Johnny crying. "What's wrong now?" said the conductor. "It was 20p I lost and you didn't give me any change". The conductor said, "Show me your ticket". Then he stopped the bus. "Now", he said, "you get out and walk home, and the next time anyone is kind to you, try to show a little gratitude". As wee Johnny walked along the road he was a very humble little boy and that day he learned a lesson that he never forgot - always to be grateful for the goodness of others.

(Gratitude)

The lighthouse

Boys and girls, when wee Johnny was away on holiday he often stood at night and watched the lighthouse which sent its great beam of light across the sea.

The lighthouse was at the end of a long peninsula and it must have been about 8 miles away from the caravan park where Johnny was staying and yet the light flashed brightly. I'm sure if you were out at sea you could have seen it for 15 to 20 miles. Johnny thought it must be a very powerful light to be able to pierce the darkness and make itself seen at such a great distance. One day Johnny's Daddy said, "Would you like to visit the lighthouse?" "Of course I would", said Johnny, so they drove to the lighthouse and were shown all over it. Johnny expected to see a terrific lamp but instead he saw 5 tiny little glass jets which were not much stronger than five candles. The secret was that around the lights there was built a cage of glass, magnifying glass so that the tiny lights were multiplied many hundreds of times. The tiny lights became a brilliant light because they were magnified by the glass.

Sometimes we think we are so small and powerless that we are not able to help. And so we are, if we depend on ourselves; but let your life be surrounded by Jesus and our weakness becomes power and our little efforts become magnified a thousand times. "Ye are the light of the world", said Jesus. But our light is so feeble that it will never be seen unless we let it shine through Jesus and then we will be really bright lights in the darkness.

(Light of the world: 2 Corinthians ch. 12 v. 9)

Telephone No. 1690

One day wee Johnny was very excited at school because they were getting in the telephone at home and he would be able to phone his friends. The man from the Post Office had been at the house and the wiring was complete. He said the telephone no. would be 1690. Johnny thought he would have no trouble remembering that number. Johnny told his friends that the man from the Post Office thought the number would be 1690 - "Don't forget the number - remember 1690".

At last the great day came when the phone was connected and when Johnny looked at the number he couldn't believe it. It wasn't 1690, but it was 316. There must be some mistake he thought. It was such a disappointment. There must be some way of remembering 316 thought Johnny. All at once he had a great idea. "I have it", he shouted with delight. "My name - and then the number. Not Johnny, but my proper name - John 3:16/ The most beautiful text in the Bible".

I'm sure none of you will forget Johnny's telephone number and I hope you will never forget John 3:16. "For God so loved the world that He gave His only begotten Son that whosoever believeth in Him should not perish, but have everlasting life".

(Twelfth of July: John ch. 3 v. 16)

Johnny's bill

One day Johnny's Mammy sent him to the butcher for a pound of steak. Johnny said to the butcher, "I want a pound of steak, please, and give it to me tough".

"That's strange", said the butcher, "most people ask for tender steak". "Well", answered Johnny, "if it's tender my Daddy would eat it all".

Of course Johnny was only joking. He knew that the most unselfish people in the world were his parents. He had once learned how much his Daddy and Mammy had done for him in a way he never forgot. He sent a bill to his Mammy and this is what it said:-

For tidying my bedroom	20p
For running messages	20p
For brushing the floor	20p
For cleaning shoes	20p
For looking after baby	20p
Total	£1

He slipped it to his Mammy when he was going to bed. Next morning when he came down there was an envelope for him. In it there was a bill for Johnny from his Mammy.

Clothes for 8 years	0
Food for 8 years	0
Holidays and toys	0
Pocket money for 8 years	0
Total	0

When Johnny read it he felt ashamed and there and then he made up his mind that, in future, he would do his very best to show his gratitude for what his Mammy and Daddy had done for him. It would be great if all the boys and girls in Church today would follow Johnny's example.

(Gratitude)

April fool

Last Wednesday morning wee Johnny's Mammy was busy baking in the kitchen. She was getting a cake ready for the oven when the door bell rang. She washed her hands and went to the door only to see Johnny's head disappearing round the corner of the house and he shouted "April Fool". His Mammy laughed and went to the kitchen and put her cake in the oven. She went upstairs to tidy the bedrooms. After a while Johnny came up saying, "I smell something burning". His Mammy said, "My cake!" and rushed down to the oven to find everything cooking perfectly. "April Fool", said Johnny and he laughed and laughed.

Later on his Mammy said, "Johnny would you do a message for me please?" Go to Mr. Todd's shop and ask him for 'The Long Stand'". "But I don't know what it's like", said Johnny. "Don't worry", said his Mammy, "Mr. Todd knows what it is".

Johnny went to the shop and asked for "The Long Stand". Mr. Todd called the message boy and said, "Go down to the store and get 'The Long Stand'". Johnny waited and waited and waited. Then he said to Mr. Todd, "What's keeping him?" "Are you tired standing?" said Mr. Todd. "I am", said Johnny. "Well", said Mr. Todd, "Go home and tell your Mammy you got 'The Long Stand' and her April Fool worked".

"April Fool", said his Mammy when he got home. But Johnny said, "That's not much of a trick" and he went away and sulked all day.

But that night when he went to bed his Mammy came in to talk to him and Johnny learned a lesson he never forgot. He learned that while it's a good thing to be able to laugh at a joke, it is far better to be able to laugh when the joke is against you.

(April Fool: Ephesians ch. 4 v. 26)

Johnny up in an aeroplane

This summer wee Johnny was up in an aeroplane. He was very excited about it and he just loves to talk about it. He was telling his friends all about the take off, the climb up into the heavens, the passage through the clouds and the beauty of the clear sky above. When he was finished they were asking all kinds of questions. "What speed were you doing?" "What height were you up?" Johnny was able to answer all the questions like a pilot who had made 1,000 flights. "Tell me", said one of his friends, "when you were away up that height, did you see God?" "Not at all", said Johnny, "We weren't nearly high enough for that".

Whether Johnny expected to see God or not I don't know. But I do know we can see God without going up in an aeroplane. We can see Him best of all by looking at Jesus. He is shown to us in the pages of the New Testament. Jesus came into the world not only to save the world but to show us what God is like and through reading the story of His life we know that God is love.

Of course there are thousands of boys and girls in the world who do not know what God is like because they have never heard of Jesus. That is why we send missionaries to tell people the good news that God is love. Wouldn't it be great if there was a boy or girl in Church today who would give their life to the service of God as a doctor or nurse, a teacher or a preacher to tell those who have never heard it, that God is love.

(Seeing God: Colossians ch. 1 v. 15)

Johnny and the umbrella

One day wee Johnny's Daddy came home at lunch time and he was in a terrible hurry. He was rushing because he was going to a funeral and he hadn't much time. He had only half an hour to take his lunch, change his clothes, get dressed and get out. And so he had everyone dancing attendance on him. "Here Johnny", he said, "take my shoes and polish them". Then he asked Johnny's Mammy to brush his black coat while he ran upstairs and changed. It wasn't long until he was down again. He put on the shoes Johnny had shined, rushed out to the hall and put on his coat and hat.

"Here are your gloves", said Johnny's Mammy "Where is your umbrella?" "Run upstairs Johnny", said his Daddy, "and see if it's in the wardrobe in my bedroom?" Johnny was up the stairs, two at a time and down again quick as lightning but he had no umbrella. "Is it not there?" asked his Daddy. "It's there all right, just where you said", answered Johnny. "Well why didn't you bring it down?" asked his Daddy. "You didn't tell me to", said Johnny, "You only asked me to see if it was in the wardrobe!" But before his Daddy could say anything Johnny was up and down again with the umbrella with a great big smile all over his face. Of course Johnny was only joking and that evening they all laughed at Johnny's little trick.

You know that's the sort of thing we all do in life. We are very careful never to do more than we are asked to do. You remember the words of Jesus - if any man ask you to go with him a mile - go with him two miles. Don't be content, said Jesus, with doing only what you have to do or what you're expected to do. Always be ready and willing to do a little more. Will you remember that the next time you are asked to do something at home.

(The second mile: Matthew ch. 5 vs. 40-42)

What God has joined together

One day in Sunday School the lesson was on the Ten Commandments. The teacher went to a great deal of trouble to explain how the commandments had been given by God to Moses for the children of Israel, and how they were meant to be kept not only by them but by all men in all ages. "Now", said the teacher, "let us see how the Commandments affect our lives". She began to ask them questions. She turned to the boy at the end of the row, "Suppose some day you are playing an exciting game and in the middle of it your Mammy asks you to do a message and you refuse to do it - what Commandment would you be breaking?" "The fifth", came the answer, "Honour thy Father and thy Mother". "Right", said the teacher. Then she asked the next boy, "Suppose some day you are at home on your own and you know there is a box of chocolates in the cupboard which you are not allowed to touch. You take one and eat it, thinking it will never be missed. What Commandment would you be breaking?" "The eighth, 'Thou shalt not steal'". "Right", said the teacher.

Then it came to wee Johnny's turn - "Suppose one day you caught a fly and you took off a wing to see if it could fly with one wing. then you took off a leg to see if it could walk with 3 legs, then you took off all its legs. Finally you tramped it on the floor under your foot. What Commandment would you be breaking?" Wee Johnny couldn't think of a Commandment. He didn't remember the sixth commandment and then wee Johnny had a brain wave. "I know a text from the Bible". "What is it?" said the teacher. Johnny said, "What God has joined together, let not man put asunder!"

We can learn many lessons from this story. Firstly, never be cruel to any of God's creatures, even a fly. Also, remember that the

Commandments, in spite of their great age, still have a message for us today.

I want you to remember a chapter from the Old Testament written especially for young people - Ecclesiastes ch. 12.

"Remember now thy creator in the days of thy youth". The chapter ends - "Fear God and keep His Commandments, for this is the whole duty of man".

And when you think of the 10 Commandments, never forget the two which Jesus added - "Thou shalt love the Lord thy God and thy neighbour as thyself".

(Ten Commandments: Ecclesiastes ch. 12 v. 13; Matthew ch. 19 v. 6)

"God loveth a cheerful giver"

One Sunday at wee Johnny's Church there was a special collection for world development - to help to feed the hungry people of the world. On Sunday morning Johnny reminded his Daddy about it. "I hadn't forgotten", said his Daddy, "and as well as your ordinary envelope I want you to give something special too" and he reached him two coins. "One of those is for yourself", said his Daddy, "The other is for the special collection". When Johnny looked at them he saw that one was a 10p piece and the other a 50p piece.

"I suppose I needn't ask which is for me", said Johnny. "No indeed", said his Daddy, "You needn't ask, for I'm not going to tell you. I'm going to leave it to you. You can give whichever you like to the collection and you can keep the other for yourself".

Wasn't that a terrible situation for any wee boy to be in? I wonder what you would have done if you had been in Johnny's place? What do you think Johnny did? Well, when they came home from Church his Daddy asked him. "You know", said Johnny, "I had a terrible struggle. It wasn't easy to decide. I thought of nothing else all the time in Church. And it wasn't until just before the collection I made up my mind. I didn't really want to give the 50p, but I felt I ought to give it. I would have been quite glad to give the 10p but I thought that would be mean. Just then I thought of a text which solved the whole problem". "What was it?" asked his Daddy. Johnny said, "It was - 'God loveth a cheerful giver' and I was cheerful when I gave the 10p piece".

"Well", said his Daddy, "that's your decision but answer me one question - were you really cheerful - really happy, when you gave the 10p piece?" "To tell you the truth", said Johnny, "I wasn't happy at all". His Daddy never mentioned it again but next Sunday there was an envelope on the plate with a 50p piece in it. Written on the envelope was - "For the world development collection - from a really cheerful giver". It is more blessed to give than to receive.

(Offering: 2 Corinthians ch. 9 v. 7; Acts ch. 20 v. 35)

Johnny bathing

When wee Johnny was away on his holidays he was a great bather. He just loved the sea and every day he had a swim. Indeed some days he had a swim 2 or 3 times.

But one morning at breakfast he was coughing and sneezing and his Daddy said, "I think Johnny you had better not bathe today". "Ah, why not", said Johnny, "Sure everyone bathes".

"Not today", said his Daddy and that was that. But at lunchtime when his Daddy was coming up from the beach - he spied Johnny slipping into the house. He had a pair of wet bathing trunks in his hands. "I thought I told you not to bathe", said his Daddy and he was really cross. "I didn't mean to bathe", said Johnny, "but I was going down to the pool to meet some of the boys and I thought I should take my togs with me, in case I was tempted". Just imagine, "in case I was tempted" - wouldn't you think wee Johnny would have more sense. I hope none of you encourage temptation like that. That only makes it easier to fall and, dear knows, it is easy enough.

It tells us in the Bible "Resist the devil and he will flee from you". Remember that and remember too that the best way to overcome temptation is to seek God's help. So next time you are told not to do something you want to do - or told to do something you don't want to do, ask God to help you. Shut your eyes and ears to temptation. That way you will find it easier to be true to God and obedient to those who love you.

*(Temptation:
1 Corinthians
ch. 10 v. 13)*

Palm Sunday

Today is Palm Sunday - that is the Sunday before Easter when Jesus went in triumph into the city of Jerusalem. It gets its name because the people broke the branches off the palm trees and waved them in welcome to the King. You remember how they shouted out "Hosanna" and spread their garments in His path while He rode in majesty upon a colt "whereon never man sat" - a colt which had never been ridden before.

One day a missionary was reading the story of Palm Sunday to a group of cowboys. They listened in silence to every word of it, because they had never heard it before. When the story was finished one of the cowboys stood up and said, "What a wonderful man He must have been". "Why do you say that?" asked the missionary. "Well", said the cowboy, "a man who could sit on a colt which no-one had ridden before and could ride it quietly with people shouting and waving palms all around Him - He must have been a wonderful man".

And so He was but He was more than that. He was the son of a wonderful God. A God whose love for us is shown in countless different ways every day we live. God's greatest love for us is shown this week, because this is Easter week and Friday is Good Friday, the day Christ was crucified on the cross. As we remember the wonder of God's love for us, may we be grateful for that love, and may we show our gratitude by opening our hearts that Christ may come and live in us.

(Palm Sunday)

Johnny and the slides

There was a man in Johnny's Church who had a cine camera. He was making a film all about the village and the countryside around the Church. When he had it finished he showed it in the Church hall. Everyone was so interested in it that the hall was packed. They all enjoyed seeing the pictures on the screen of the village, the Church, the school and lots of people they knew. Johnny was shouting out "Oh there's Willie's house" or "There's Tommy's house". "Look Mammy there's Jimmy's wee sister and there's old Mr. Brown". He was so excited when he saw pictures of the Sunday School picnic. Then there came on the screen a little boy with a big cross face. "Who's that Mammy", he said. "That's you Johnny", said his Mammy. Poor Johnny couldn't believe it! He never thought that he could look so cross but right enough it was himself. "You see", said his Mammy, "you couldn't see yourself as others see you".

How many of us are like that? If only we could see our faces when we are cross I don't think we would ever be cross again. If only we could see ourselves when we do something naughty. If only we could see ourselves the way God sees us we would be very sorry for all the sinful things we do and we would try our best not to do them again.

(Our reflection)

The best time to pray

This year when wee Johnny was on holiday in Portrush he met a wee boy from Scotland. His name was Iain and soon they became good friends. It's wonderful what wee boys talk about when they are alone. Well Johnny and Iain talked about everything under the sun. One day they began to talk about religion, church and Sunday school. Then out of the blue Iain asked this question - "When is the best time of the day to say your prayers?" "I suppose in the morning, at the beginning of the day", said Johnny. "I think the evening is better", said Iain. "Why do you think that?" Johnny asked. "Well", Iain replied, "according to the Post Office it is cheaper to send messages at night".

It's like the time wee Johnny asked his Daddy - "What's the cheapest time to phone your friends?" "After six, from Monday to Friday or any time on Saturday or Sunday", answered his Daddy. "No", said Johnny, "The cheapest time to phone your friends is when they are out".

Now there are two lessons about prayer we can learn from this. The first is God is never out. He doesn't work from 9 to 5 with the weekend off. He doesn't even take a half day. He is on call 24 hours a day, 7 days a week, year after year after year. That is what is meant when we talk about God's ear always being open to our cry. So we can pray at any time and be sure that God is always listening.

The second lesson is about the charge for a call to God. How much is it? Nothing, it is a "free phone". There is no charge. Isn't it a pity we don't use the line more often. Tennyson, the poet wrote "more things are wrought by prayer than this world dreams of".

(Prayer)

Eating an apple & saying your prayers

On Friday night wee Johnny didn't want to go to bed. Two or three times his Mammy said, "It's time you were in bed, Johnny". Johnny replied, "There's no hurry, sure there's no school in the morning and I haven't to get up early". At last his Mammy said, "Look Johnny, go to bed now, and if you like, you can take an apple with you". So Johnny picked a nice red apple and was off to bed.

The next morning he was playing with his friend Jimmy and he told him about the apple. "Will you give me a bit of it?" asked Jimmy. "It's all eaten long ago". "When did you eat it?" asked Jimmy. "I ate it last night when I was saying my prayers", answered Johnny. "You shouldn't do that", said Jimmy. "Why not?" asked Johnny. And they had an argument - was it right or wrong to eat an apple when you were saying your prayers?

To settle it they both said they would ask their Daddies next day. When they met, Jimmy said, "My Daddy says it's wrong". Johnny said, "My Daddy says it's all right". So they were as far on as ever. "I can't understand how your Daddy says it's all right", said Jimmy. "Well you see", said Johnny, "it all depends on how you ask the question. You probably asked your Daddy, 'Is it all right to eat an apple when you are praying ?' and your Daddy said 'No'. But I asked my Daddy 'Is it all right to pray when you are eating an apple?' and of course he said 'Yes'".

So there you are, and what can you make of that? Well I think we can learn a good lesson from it about prayer. That although you can pray to God, at any time and in any place, no matter what you are doing, yet it is a good thing to set apart a time of every day when you do nothing else or think of nothing else but God.

(Prayer: Matthew ch. 6 v. 6)

The cricket

Boys and girls I want to tell you about a man who lived in the country and was a great lover of nature. He knew all the trees by their names. He knew the names of the birds and all their different songs. He could tell you the names of all the wild flowers. He once went on a visit to a city and there, just by accident, he met a friend on a busy street and they began to talk.

Hundreds of people were hurrying past. The buses and cars were making a great noise. Suddenly the country visitor stopped talking. "Hush", he said, "listen, I hear a cricket". His friend laughed at him. "How could you hear a cricket in all this noise?" he asked. The country man walked over to a window box with flowers in it and sure enough there was the cricket, chirping merrily away. "How on earth did you hear it?" asked his friend. "I hear it", came the answer, "because I have used my ears since boyhood listening to nature. People in the city wouldn't notice the cricket but wait to you see this". He put his hand in his pocket and took out a coin and dropped it on the footpath. Immediately, about twenty people stopped and looked down to the ground. You see their ears were listening for the sound of money, but not one of them heard the cricket.

The lesson of that story is that if we are too busy with the world then we miss the still small voice of God.

Train your ears to listen to God for He often wants to speak to you and if you miss His voice you will miss one of the greatest things in life.

(Listening to God; Money: Matthew ch. 6 v. 24)

That's powerful (Whit)

There's a word which wee Johnny uses very often. You and I know what it means and so do all Johnny's friends.

But one time there was a boy at Johnny's school who had come from America. His name was Keith. He couldn't understand this word at all. One day he asked Johnny, "What is this world 'powerful' which you are always using? What does it mean? Whenever it's raining you say 'it's powerful wet', when the sun is shining you say 'it's powerful hot' and when the wind is blowing you say 'it's powerful windy'. I can't understand how you can use the same word for all those different things". "Do you mean to say you don't know what powerful means?" asked Johnny. "No", answered Keith. "Boys", said Johnny, "that's powerful".

It's a great word 'powerful', one which I often use myself. I am telling you this today because this is a powerful day, in every sense of the word.

I don't mean that it is powerful hot or wet. I mean simply that it's powerful. This is Whit Sunday and it is a powerful day because it was on this day that the Holy Spirit came into the lives of the first disciples and filled them with Power.

Because of that they were able to do the most wonderful things. Because the power of God filled their hearts, fear was driven away and they set out into the world proclaiming that Jesus had risen from the dead and was alive for evermore. This is the secret of all the great things we read about in the book of Acts.

This is the secret of the great apostle Paul, and of the lives of great Christians in all ages. They were filled with the power of the Holy Spirit and because of that they were ready for anything. God has promised that if we ask Him, He will fill us with power and make us able to do all things - isn't that powerful?

(Whit Sunday; Holy Spirit: Acts ch. 1 v. 8; Philippians ch. 4 v. 13)

How much to be honest

One day wee Johnny's Mammy went to Belfast on the bus and that evening Johnny and his Daddy went to the Bus Station to meet her coming home. When Johnny's Mammy got off the bus she had a lot of parcels but Johnny noticed something she hadn't got. "Where is your handbag?" he asked. "Oh", said his Mammy, "I must have left it on the bus". So she rushed immediately back to the bus to look for it. But before she got to the bus she met the driver and he had her bag in his hand.

"Is this what you are looking for?" he asked. "It is indeed", she said, "Thank you very much. I thought maybe one of the passengers might have taken it".

The driver gave her the bag and then he made a rather unusual request. "Would you mind telling me how much money you have in it", he asked. "Why do you want to know that?" replied Johnny's Mammy. "I'll tell you in a minute", said the driver. Johnny's Mammy opened her purse and began to count her money. "I have £12.75", she said. The driver took out a little note book and he wrote the date, then £12.75. Then he showed the note book to Johnny's Mammy and there was a page of dates and figures. When the figures were all added up the total came to over £250. "You see that", said the driver, "that's all the money I have found and given back to the owners - that is how much it cost me to be honest".

You know you can't really count in pounds and pence the value of a good name, or the value of a clear conscience. It says in the book of Proverbs "A good name is better than precious ointment" and there is another proverb which says, "Honesty is the best policy". Both are very true. I hope you will remember that and try in all your dealings to do what is upright and honest.

(Honesty: Proverbs ch. 22 v. 1)

The Book of Life

When we were on holiday we went to the beautiful little Presbyterian Church at Dunfanaghy. Visitors are always very welcome and they keep a 'Visitors' Book' in which visitors can write their names and addresses. We haven't got a Visitors' Book in Edenderry, but we have a number of other books with names and addresses. I am sure your name is in some of them. Every baby who is baptised has its name entered in a book by the minister, with the name of the parents and the date of birth. Every boy and girl in Sunday School has his name in the Sunday School Roll Book. Every person who comes to Communion has his name in the Communion Roll Book. Then every person who is married in Church has to sign the Marriage Book. And those who give money for the work of the Church have their names printed every year in the Financial Statement.

It is a good thing to be connected with the Church and to have your name entered in the books. But there is one book, above all, in which it is most important that your name should be written. It is called the 'Book of Life'. It is kept by God in heaven. In that Book are written the names of all who belong to God. This is a great book in which God keeps the names of all those who, in this life, accept the way of Christ and who love and serve and follow him.

(Book of Life: Philippians ch. 4 v. 3)

When you come and give your life to Jesus, your name will be entered in the 'Book of Life'.

Finding a pound coin

One day wee Johnny and his best friend Jimmy were walking up the street. Suddenly they both dashed forward and dived headlong on the footpath. What do you think had happened? They had both seen something lying on the footpath and from the distance it looked very like a pound coin. And so indeed it was. When they scrambled to their feet again wee Johnny had the pound coin clasped firmly in his hand. "What will you do with it?" asked Jimmy. "I'll put it in my money box and keep it for my holidays", answered Johnny. "What about sharing it with me?" suggested Jimmy, "after all we both saw it at the same time. I think we should go into partnership". "Alright", said Johnny, "we'll go into partnership. I'll keep this one, and the next one we find you can keep it".

Well, that wasn't a very generous offer, for it's not every day you find a pound coin. When Johnny got home he told his Mammy about finding the pound coin and about the partnership with Jimmy. He was to keep the next one they found.

"Well, I'm very disappointed with you", said his Mammy, "You are very selfish. For one thing the coin doesn't belong to you. You should take it to the police and they will try to find the owner and if nobody claims it they will give it back to you.But apart from that I don't think much of your arrangement with your friend Jimmy and I'm sure he doesn't either. You should have shared with him at once". That was all she said but that night wee Johnny took a 50p piece out of his money box and didn't put in the pound coin. Next morning he gave Jimmy the 50p and at the school dinner hour he took the pound coin to the police station. The policeman took his name and address and told him if it wasn't claimed it would be returned to him. That night it was a very happy boy that got into Johnny's bed because he had learned the truth of what Jesus said "It is more blessed to give than to receive".

*(Fairness;
Sharing:
Acts ch. 20 v. 35)*

Admitting you are wrong

Not long along wee Johnny learned a new trick. Since then he has tried it lots of times and it nearly always works. If you listen very carefully you'll hear how to do it and you'll be able to try it on your friends - that is, of course, if they are not here today. Let me tell you how Johnny worked it with his Daddy. He held out his hand with two 10p pieces on it. "Look, Daddy", he said, "I've got three coins on my hand". "No you have not", said his Daddy, "you've only got two". "I say I've got three", said Johnny, "I say you've only got two", replied his Daddy.

"Then you say I'm wrong", said Johnny. "Of course you're wrong", said his Daddy. "Will you give me 10p if I'm wrong?" "Yes", said his Daddy. "Alright", answered Johnny, "I am wrong". Although his Daddy was annoyed at his own stupidity, he paid up as promised, and Johnny was a very happy boy.

Of course Johnny doesn't always admit he's wrong as easily or as gladly as that. You know it's a good thing to have the grace to admit you have made a mistake, although sometimes it's not easy to do. You all know the story of the Prodigal Son. You remember what he had to do before he could come home and make it up with his father. He had to admit he had made a mistake. "I will arise and go to my father, and will say to him, 'Father I have sinned'".

And you remember how when he did that his father received him with open arms and welcomed him back to his place in the family.

Now that's something we all have to do before God can receive us back and give us a place in His family. We have to admit we have made a mistake; we have to say "Father I have sinned". And when we do that in sincerity, God receives us with open arms.

(Repentance: Luke ch. 15 v. 18)

No talking in Church

When wee Johnny started coming to Church his Mammy always kept saying to him, "Remember Johnny no talking in Church". Usually he wasn't too bad. But his Mammy always said every Sunday morning, "Remember Johnny, no talking in Church". Johnny didn't miss many Sundays at Church and when it came to Prize Sunday he was there and was very excited. Johnny waited a long time and watched the boys and girls go up for their prizes. At last his name was called, so he marched up to the front and got his book from the minister. He got it for good attendance and Johnny was very pleased. When they got home his Mammy looked at his prize and she said, "Well done Johnny, I hope you said thank you to the minister". "I didn't", said Johnny, "because I'm not allowed to talk in Church".

What could his Mammy say to that? We shouldn't talk to each other in Church but this is the one place, above all others, where we should talk to God. For this is God's house and we come especially to meet Him. Although we can't see God we can talk to Him and He can talk to us. God talks to us in the prayers, the hymns, maybe in the reading of the Bible, or the sermon. God talks to us in a still small voice and we have to be very quiet if we want to hear His voice.

God is saying to us now "This is my house, this is the place of prayer, come in quietness and I will meet with you and talk with you". God has promised "Where two or three are gathered together in my name I am in the midst of them".

(Worship: Matthew ch. 18 v. 20)

Happy
Congrat
It's your
BiRTHDA
HAPPY
BiRTH
DAY

Be ready

Last week there was a party at wee Johnny's house because it was his birthday. There were ten boys and girls at the party, all of them friends of Johnny's. After Johnny had opened his presents the children started to play games - all the usual games that boys and girls play at a party. Then they had a lovely tea and after tea they had a video. When the video was over there was still some time left so Johnny's Mammy suggested they should have a concert.

They all entered into it quite happily. One of the girls sang, and then a boy said a poem. Then Johnny's special friend Jimmy played the piano. Then everybody said that wee Johnny would have to do something himself and, all of a sudden, Johnny got very shy. At last they persuaded him to play the piano too. So Johnny got up and sat at the piano and called over to his Mammy, "What will I play? You tell me what to play?" "Don't be a baby", said his Mammy, "Sure Jimmy hadn't to ask his Mammy what to play".

"No indeed", said Jimmy, "I practised what I was going to play before I came". "How did you know you were going to be asked to play?" shouted Johnny. "Now, now", said his Mammy, "Jimmy was right. It's always a good thing to be ready".

And so it is. It tells us that in the Bible. It tells us in Acts that Paul was ready not only to be bound, but even to die for Jesus. Peter tells us in his Epistle to be ready to give an answer to everyone that asketh the reason for our faith. It's a good thing to be able to do that. The best example of all is in the words of Jesus Himself - "Be ye also ready". And the way to be ready is just to open our hearts to Jesus, and commit our lives entirely to His care. When we do that we are ready, really ready, for anything.

(Ready, Second Coming: Matthew ch. 24 v. 44, Acts ch. 21 v. 13, 1 Peter ch. 3 v. 15)

The duck's waddle

Wee Johnny wasn't very keen on doing his homework and, every evening, his Mammy had to keep at him and at him to do his homework. I'm sure it's the same boys and girls in some of your homes.

Well today I want to tell you about the duck's waddle. A duck has a funny walk. It's really awkward looking and we call it a waddle. When it comes to the water it sails silently along, full of ease and grace, for it is much more at home in the water. It is said that ducks and geese were once, long ago, much more land birds than they are now and then they could walk gracefully. But they grew fonder and fonder of the water and used their legs more and more for swimming and less for walking until now they can only waddle. The same thing happened to other birds such as the kiwi. It once had wings to fly but it grew lazy and its wings got smaller and smaller, until now it has hardly any wings and cannot fly.

The powers you do not use you lose. If you never exercise your muscles, they grow weak and flabby. If you never use your brain to think, you will grow dull and stupid. If you never try to be good and kind, you soon become unreliable and unpleasant. It is one of God's laws. Only by using the powers He has given you, can they be kept strong. God made us to walk straight and strong in the ways of goodness and truth, but there are plenty of people who have lost the power to do that because they have stopped trying.

Boys and girls, learn a lesson from the duck and the kiwi. Don't lose the powers that God has given you to serve Him in the world.

(Talents: Romans ch. 12 vs. 6-8)

They shall not all sleep

During the summer, wee Johnny was visiting his cousin and in his Church they were going to start a nursery in the Church hall. The idea was that parents who have babies too young to come to Church could leave them with the people in charge of the nursery.

At the service on Sunday the minister told the boys and girls about the nursery. They were getting a special room ready, nicely furnished and painted. They wanted to paint a special text from the Bible over the door.

The minister said he wanted all the boys and girls to send in a suggestion and he would give a prize to the most original one. They were to write it on a card and say where it came from.

Some boys and girls wrote: "Suffer the little children to come unto me".

One wrote: "Train up a child in the way he should go" - Proverbs 22 : 6

Another wrote: "What manner of child shall this be" - Luke 1 : 66

I'm sure you would never guess the text wee Johnny sent in. If it wasn't the most suitable it certainly was the most original. He thought of all the babies in the nursery, in their prams and carry cots. Some of them would be asleep and some awake. Johnny's suggestion was: "They shall not all sleep - but they shall all be changed" - 1 Corinthians 15 verse 51.

Of course this verse isn't really about babies at all. It's about the great promise that everyone who loves the Lord shall be changed so that we can live with Him for ever.

*(Our resurrection:
1 Corinthians
ch. 15 v. 51)*

I love it- I love you - St. Valentine's Day

This is the story of four teenagers - Jimmy, Jean, Harry and Hilda. As you might guess, Jimmy had a crush on Jean and Harry had a crush on Hilda. On Friday the two boys saw the two girls home from school and then went back into town to buy presents for the girls for Valentine's Day.

Jimmy had plenty of money but Harry was nearly broke. Jimmy went to the jeweller's and bought a pair of expensive earrings. Harry went to Wellworths and bought a nice embroidered handkerchief. Jimmy wrapped his gift in fancy paper and put it inside a big heart shaped card and wrote "From Jimmy".

Harry couldn't even afford a Valentine card so he got a plain card and wrote on it:

If I were wealthy as a Prince with endless stores of gold
With gems and jewels glittering my love I would unfold.
This is a very simple gift - 'tis all I can afford
But it goes with sweet affection to Hilda - my adored.

Next day at lunch time Jimmy met Jean and she said, "Thank you for your present I love it".

Harry met Hilda and she said, "Thank you for your present 'I love you'".

Do you see the difference? "I love it" - "I love you". One is impersonal and cold - the other is affectionate and personal. It teaches us that while it is important to appreciate a gift - it is more important to appreciate the giver. We should try to remember that in life - especially when we are young, because we receive so many gifts from those who love us. We should show our gratitude by giving our love in return. We should learn to look on all God's gifts as tokens of His love for us and we should express our love to God, not only in words but in our lives from day to day.

(St. Valentine's Day)

10p for Church - 10p for sweets

Wee Johnny has two very fixed habits on Sunday - one of them is good, the other is, well, not so good.

Every Sunday he goes to Sunday School and Church - that's the good habit. Every Sunday on his way to Sunday School he buys a packet of sweets to suck in Church - that's not such a good habit. He has done this since he was a wee boy and every Sunday morning his Daddy gives him two 10p pieces - one for Church and one for sweets. One Sunday as he walked along the road he dropped one of his 10p pieces. It rolled away in front of him down a grating and disappeared. Johnny kneeled down and looked into the grating but there was no sign of his money and be began to cry. Just then a man came along the road and saw him. He stopped and asked what was wrong.

"I've lost my money for Church", sobbed Johnny. The man helped Johnny to look for it and then he saw the 10p piece in Johnny's hand. "Look", he said, "you have your collection in your hand". "Oh no", said Johnny, "That's not my collection for Church, that's my 10p for sweets".

Now if you had been wee Johnny I wonder which 10p you would have lost. If you had one coin for Church and one for yourself - which would it be?

I know it would be very nice to keep what you have for yourself but it is more unselfish and more like Jesus to forget about yourself and make a little sacrifice.

This is just what God did when he wanted to give us a gift - He gave His only son and Jesus gave Himself for us. Surely none of us can ever do too much for Him.

(Offering; Priorities: Acts ch. 20 v. 35)

Christmas - looking in the wrong place

Wee Johnny went to bed without being asked on Christmas Eve. He had a bath and put on clean pyjamas and he was all excited. He had written a letter to Santa and he had asked for a number of things. He had no doubt Santa would come when he was asleep and leave the presents in his bedroom. But Johnny was so excited that he was awake very early in the morning - long before anyone else. He switched on the light and looked around the room but there were no presents from Santa. Then he began to think of all the other boys and girls Santa had to call on and he thought that maybe Santa hadn't got the length of his house yet. So he settled down in bed again and after a while he fell fast asleep and didn't waken until the morning.

When he woke up, he looked all round his room, but there were no presents. So he rushed downstairs and his Mammy was in the kitchen. "Happy Christmas Johnny", she said and Johnny just burst into tears. "He didn't come to me", he sobbed, "Santa didn't come". "Look", said his Mammy, "Did you look in the living room?"

In two ticks, Johnny was in the living room and there on the hearth rug were all the things he had asked for. "You see Johnny", said his Mammy, "you were looking in the wrong place. You made the same mistake as the three wise men who set out to find the baby Jesus. They couldn't find him at first because they were looking in the wrong place. He was a king and they thought he would be born in a palace. But they found him in a stable at an inn. There they found the most wonderful Christmas present that ever was - the unspeakable gift of Jesus".

The secret of all happiness at Christmas and all the time is to look in the right place. For happiness is not found in the things of the world like money and pleasure. Those who look for it there are looking in the wrong place. True happiness can only be found in God and His kingdom, by serving others and loving Jesus.

(Christmas: Matthew ch. 2 vs. 1-2; Matthew ch. 7 v. 7)

Two corncrakes

This is the story of two corncrakes who had their nest in a field of corn. One was an old corncrake, the other was young.

One evening the young corncrake overheard the farmer and his son talking. "The corn is ripe", said the farmer, "and the weather's good. It's time it was cut. Run down to Willie John's and ask him to come in the morning and cut it".

The young corncrake rushed back and told the old corncrake. "I think we better pack up and go", he said. "No", answered the old corncrake, "not yet". And sure enough the morning came and nothing happened.

Next night the farmer and his son were talking and the farmer said to his son, "Willie John didn't come, go and ask Bob Sam if he would come in the morning to cut the corn".

The young corncrake rushed back to the old corncrake to tell him. The old corncrake said, "Time enough to go yet".

The third night the young corncrake overheard the farmer say to his son, "It's a pity Willie John and Bob Sam couldn't come but you be here early in the morning and we'll cut the corn ourselves".

When the young corncrake told the old corncrake this, the old corncrake said, "Right we'll go tonight" and, sure enough, the next day the corn was cut.

I hope none of you, boys and girls, will be like Willie John and Bob Sam, the kind of people you can't depend on. If you are asked to do anything for others and promise to do it - then at all costs, keep your word.

If you do that you will be loyal to your friends, true to yourself and faithful to God.

(Trustworthiness; Harvest)

A bad impression

One day wee Johnny was going home from school in the bus and he was very badly behaved. He had a real wrestling match with the boy on the seat beside him. He took another boy's cap and threw it away up the bus. He kept making cheeky remarks about people they passed on the road. Indeed he made a complete nuisance of himself, and when the bus came to the stop where he got off, everyone breathed a sigh of relief. He swung his schoolbag over his shoulder, put his coat over his arm, picked up his cap and scarf and shouted, "Cheerio". But before the bus moved off, the driver called him back. "Here, Johnny, you have left something behind". Johnny took a quick look at his belongings. He had his bag, coat, cap and scarf. "I haven't left anything behind", he shouted back. "Oh yes you have", replied the driver, "you have left a very bad impression".

You see, although Johnny had all his belongings he left behind him the impression of a boy who was badly behaved; a boy who was selfish and who had no consideration for others.

Now boys and girls, you know there are some boys and girls who leave a bad impression not in a bus, which is bad enough, but in Church which is a hundred times worse.

You know that's what you do when you talk and are badly behaved during the service. Apart from the annoyance it causes to the people beside you, it shows that you have little respect for God. We should never forget that this Church is God's house. When you come here we should never do anything to disturb others or to grieve the heart of God.

I hope you will all make up your minds today, that never again when you leave this Church will you leave behind a bad impression.

(Worship)

The Victoria Cross

During the 1939-45 war a famous journalist was standing at the door of an hotel in London. In front of him, near the footpath, stood the hotel commissioner or doorman. He was an old man and he had on a commissioner's uniform. The hotel was near the War Office and many high ranking officers passed it every day. The strange thing was that all the officers that passed by saluted the old commissioner. The journalist wondered at the reason for this but as soon as he spoke to the old man he knew why. On his coat the old man had many medal ribbons and among them the pride of place was given to a plain red ribbon. It was the ribbon of the Victoria Cross and when any soldier has won that award he is entitled to be saluted by all other soldiers, whatever their rank. Queen Victoria first made this unique award to mark the outstanding courage of some of her soldiers in the Crimean War.

It has been awarded ever since. It is the highest honour any member of the forces can be awarded and is given for outstanding courage. That is why officers salute the man who wears the V.C. because courage is a virtue everyone respects.

Now there are many kinds of courage. Some courage doesn't win medals on the battle field. It is what we call moral courage. It takes courage to stand up for Jesus and to be loyal to Him. It takes courage sometimes to tell the truth and to admit that you have made a mistake. It takes courage to defend what you know to be right. The secret of courage is to have the love of God in your heart. It says in the Bible "Perfect love casteth out fear". Christian courage gets no medals but it is always honoured by God and those who are faithful to Him will, one day, receive the greatest of all great awards - "Well done, thou good and faithful servant".

(Courage: 1 John ch. 4 v. 18)

Bible Sunday

I wonder how many of the boys and girls know what day it is today. Of course it's Sunday, the first Sunday of December. But it's a special Sunday - it's Bible Sunday.

Today people all over the world will be thinking of this wonderful book. You know the Bible is still the world's best seller. No other book has ever had such a place in the hearts and lives of so many people. Every year there are millions and millions of new bibles printed and circulated all over the world, in over a thousand different languages. There is one copy of the Bible I want to tell you about today. It costs a great amount of money to produce. It takes thirty nine different volumes to contain the whole Bible and when it is printed it fills a book case 7 feet long. What sort of a Bible is it? It is the Bible printed in Braille which blind people can read, not with their eyes but with their fingertips. Because it costs so much, few blind people could afford to buy it. So it is sold to the blind for very little and most of the remainder is paid by the publishers, The British and Foreign Bible Society. Some of the money collected every year from members of this congregation helps to pay for it. The Bible is not only printed in English Braille but in twenty six different languages. Many of them go to India and Pakistan where there are over two million blind people. This is only one of the wonderful things done by the Bible Society. Next time you read your Bible say a prayer for God's blessing on this work; give God thanks for His wonderful book; and rejoice that He has given you sight to read it and a mind to understand it.

Johnny and the priest

One time wee Johnny had to go into hospital to have his appendix out. Although he was really ill when he went into hospital, a couple of days after his operation he was in good form. In a few days he was up and about talking to everybody and helping the nurses in the ward.

One morning, when he was still in bed, who do you think came into the ward? It wasn't the Sister, or the Matron or the Doctor but the Priest - the Roman Catholic Priest. Johnny didn't know his name but he knew he wasn't a Presbyterian Minister. He watched him carefully and with great interest as he walked round the ward chatting to all the boys and girls. He asked them their names and where he lived and he gave everyone a sweet.

When he came to wee Johnny he asked him why he was in hospital. "Appendicitis", answered Johnny. "Where do you live?" asked the Priest. "Near Omagh", answered Johnny and then he added quickly, "I'm a Presbyterian, I don't belong to your church". "Oh, I know", said the Priest, "We both belong to different churches but we both belong to the same God".

That was the first time Johnny realised that his God and the Priest's God were one and the same person. Of course Johnny knew there were great differences between Protestants and Roman Catholics, but that day he made up his mind that, although he would always be loyal to his own church, he would never do anything, in word or deed, to create bitterness between people of different faiths.

(Roman Catholics: Luke ch. 9 vs. 49, 50)

2p piece

Boys and girls have you got a 2p piece in your pocket or purse? Take it out and have a good look at it. What can you see on it? Can you see a fruit? - I can, a date. (Calendar date - edible date).

Can you see an animal? - I can, a hair (on Queens's head - hare).

Can you see a place of worship? - I can, a temple (on Queen's head).

Well of course these are just trick questions and answers but there are four sermons on this coin and I want you to think about them.

1. The date 1971 - it is one thousand, nine hundred and seventy one years since the birth of Jesus. Every time we look at a coin we are reminded of the importance of Christ's birth.

2. In the letters round the edge of the coin there is D.G. This is short for "Dei Gratia" which means "By Grace of God". Only by God's grace is Elizabeth our Queen. This is true of all we have and all we are. (But for the grace of God we are nothing).

3. Also in the letter round the edge we see F.D. This is short for Defender of the Faith. Today the Queen at her coronation promises to defend and uphold the Protestant faith.

4. On the opposite side of the 2p coin we see the 'Fleur-De-Lys'. This is the French for Lily Flower and it is the crest of the Prince of Wales. If you have good eyesight and look carefully at the bottom you will see the words "Ich Dien". These are the German words for 'I serve" and is the motto of the Prince of Wales.

Let us try to act on these four lessons and pledge ourselves in 1971 that, by the grace of God. I will defend my faith and I will serve God and my neighbour.

(2p piece)

A man, a boy and a donkey

Boys and girls I want to tell you a story about a man, a boy and a donkey and it's as old as the hills. The man and the boy were father and son and they set out one day to sell the donkey at the fair. They started on their way and, before long, they met a man on the road who began to laugh. "Why are you walking," he said, "when you have a donkey to ride on?". So the father got on the donkey's back and the son walked. Soon they met another man who said, "What a lazy father to make his son walk while he rides". So the son got on the donkey and the father walked. The next man they met said, "Such a selfish son to ride and let his old father walk". So they decided they would both get on the donkey's back and they hadn't gone far when they met a fourth man. "Oh shame", he said, "Have you no mercy on the poor donkey". Then they decided to cut down a strong branch from a tree, tie the donkey to it by the heels and carry it between them on their shoulders. Wasn't this a really stupid thing to do?

There are two important lessons to learn from this story. Firstly, the impossibility of pleasing everyone and secondly the importance of having a mind of your own.

There are some boys and girls who are influenced by everyone they meet. They are led into mischief by listening to the advice of bad companions. You are all old enough to know the difference between good and bad and always have your mind made up, no matter what anyone says, to do what is right. The secret is to trust in God and get your strength from Him. Listen to the voice of God and obey it and you are on the right road to real happiness.

(Real Happiness)

Knitting

M1 S1 K1 PSSO P2 K2 TOG M1

I wonder if any of the boys or girls know what this means? Well, it's a line out of a knitting pattern and it means make 1, slip 1, knit 1, pass slip stitch over, purl 2, knit 2 together, make 1.

Today I want to give you a lesson on knitting. At least I want to teach you three simple rules.

1. Keep your eye on the pattern. This is very important. If you don't watch the pattern and follow it closely you will make all kinds of mistakes and you will finish with something you wouldn't wear. Keep your eye on the pattern. This is even more important in life. If you don't want to make a mess of it and finish up with something you are ashamed of, follow the pattern you find in the Bible, in the life and teaching of Jesus. He has given us an example to show us how to live - so keep your eyes on the pattern.

2. Keep your wool clean. You know how important this is if you are knitting something in a light colour. Never let your ball of wool roll onto the floor and make sure your hands are clean.

This is very important in life. We have to watch to keep our thoughts and words pure and clean. Impurity separates us from God and we have to strive, with God's help, to have clean hands and a pure heart.

3. Pick up all dropped stitches immediately. If you don't do that, the dropped stitch runs right down your knitting and spoils your work. A dropped stitch is a mistake and we must correct it at once. This is very important in life. If we don't correct our mistakes they become habits, and soon they will spoil our lives. There

is something I want you to do today. Look at what you are making of your life and then ask God to forgive you for the mistakes you have made and to help you to stick to the pattern. If you ask Him to help you, He will give you the power to make your life something that is beautiful.

(Knitting: Psalm 90 v. 17)

The snow

Boys and girls your sermon today is about the snow. There are four things I want you to notice about the snow. The first is the beauty of the snow. I don't mean just the beauty of the world when it is covered in white, I mean the beauty of each separate tiny snowflake. Each little particle of snow is made up of tiny crystals, each in the form of a pointed star. Often these crystals join together and they fall like perfect little flowers. This teaches us the infinite care God takes with everything He makes. The tiniest thing is made in perfect beauty.

The second thing is the warmth of the snow. I know that might seem a silly thing to say because it nips your fingers and toes. Scientists tell us that under 2 feet of snow the temperature is 40 degrees warmer than it is above. From this we learn that even things which seem hard and harsh in life have some good purpose in the plans of God.

The third thing is the power of the snow. When you see it fall softly and gently you might think it is one of the weak things of the world. Yet a snow storm can block roads and break telephone and electric wires. It is a very powerful force. We learn from this that, although we are small and often seem powerless, yet we can be strong if we link our lives with God. Lastly there is the purity of the snow. It is the whitest thing in the world, but it doesn't stay white for long. Its purity is marred by dust, dirt and traffic.

So too in life - a little child is pure but soon his purity is stained by sin. Only God can make us clean again. That is why we pray "Purge me with hyssop and I shall be clean. Wash me and I shall be whiter than snow".

(Snow: Psalm 51 v. 7)

Red Rum

One day the minister called at wee Johnny's school. It was just before Christmas and the boys and girls were making a crib. You all know what a crib is. It is a model of the stable where Jesus was born and it usually has straw on the floor, a manger for the baby and wee imitation animals standing or lying about. The minister was very interested and was going to ask a number of questions but he didn't get very far. He asked the boys and girls, "Who was born in a stable and has thousands and thousands of followers?" Quick as a shot, wee Johnny put up his hand, "Please Sir", he said, "Red Rum". So everybody laughed, including the teacher and the minister, and that was the end of the questions.

"Who was born in a stable and has thousands and thousands of followers?" Well of course the real answer that the minister wanted was Jesus. He was born in a stable and He has thousands of followers all over the world. It is a great privilege to be one of His servants and to belong to His church. I hope you will always be grateful for that and never forget that although we may belong to a small congregation, yet we belong to a world-wide fellowship of millions and millions of people who love Jesus. He was born in a stable and yet, today, Jesus has countless followers. Make sure that you are one of them.

(Christmas)

Franz Liszt

Boys and girls I want to tell you a true story about the famous Hungarian pianist and composer Franz Liszt. In Germany there was a little girl who was very poor because her parents died when she was young and left her without a penny. But she had one great gift she was a good musician and could play the piano very well.

When she was older she began to give concerts and, in this way, made her living. She got posters printed to advertise her performances and she put on them something which she knew would be a great attraction but which was untrue.

Beside her name she printed "Pupil of Franz Liszt". This was a wrong thing to do but all went well until one evening when she was signing her name in the hotel book she was shocked to see that Franz Liszt himself was staying in the hotel. She decided the only thing to do was to tell Franz Liszt everything. So she did. He asked her to play one of the pieces she was playing at her concert. When she had done that he gave her a few hints and asked her to play it again. Then he said, "I have given you a lesson and you really are a pupil of Liszt, so put on your programme that you have been assisted by your master Franz Liszt".

This story teaches us two lessons. Firstly, if we make a mistake, we should be frank, honest and confess it openly.

Secondly, it shows us how we should be kind and generous in forgiveness to those who have wronged us.

"Be kind to one another, forgiving one another even as God for Christ's sake hath forgiven you".

(Forgiving others: Ephesians ch. 4 v. 32)

Mr. Smile

I have in my hand a picture. It is a very clever picture of a man's face. Now it is a picture of a very grumpy looking man with a big beard. It reads at the top "If you want to know the difference it makes when you have a shave, turn this upside down". And when you turn it round, what a change! The old grumpy man has disappeared and in his place there is a very bright and smiling face. The same picture but it depends on how you look at it. It makes all the difference how we look at things.

Two men looked out through prison bars, one saw mud, the other stars. One hung his head in despair. He saw mud. The other raised his head in hope, and he saw stars.

Two little boys were drinking lemonade, one said, "My glass is half empty", the other one said, "My glass is half full". They both had the same amount of lemonade in their glass but one was feeling unhappy while the other was quite content. Two little sisters had a hen sitting on twelve eggs and eight of the eggs produced little chicks. One little girl cried, "The eggs are all bad except eight", while the other sister smiled and said, "The eggs are all good except four".

It all depends on how you look at it. No matter how bad things may seem there is always something to be thankful for. We should always try to see the bright side of things and keep on smiling.

"Count your blessings, name them one by one and it will surprise you what the Lord hath done".

(Count your blessings)

The man with the black beard

One Saturday morning Johnny's Daddy announced that they would go to Portrush for the day. Soon Johnny was busy helping to get ready and they left soon after 10 o'clock.

It was a lovely day and there were crowds of people everywhere. They went down to the beach and wee Johnny had a great time paddling and bathing. Then they had a picnic on the sands. There were lots of people enjoying the sunshine and Johnny was running all over the place. He came rushing over to his Daddy all excited. "Daddy", he said, "there's a man sitting over there who says that he knows you". So his Daddy sat up and looked around. "I don't see anyone I know", he answered. "But this man knows you well", said Johnny, "He says he was in the same class as you at school". "What is he like?" asked his Daddy. "He's a big man with a black beard", replied Johnny. "Don't be silly", said his Daddy, "there was nobody in my class at school with a black beard". "That's just like you Daddy", said Johnny, "you always forget that time makes changes".

"Indeed you are right Johnny, time makes changes, and I suppose as we get older we forget that". But there are some things that time does not change - things like truth, and honour and beauty, and courage and kindness, and a whole host of things which we get from God. And those things do not change because God is always the same. As it tells us in the Bible - the same yesterday, today and for ever.

When Johnny was saying his prayers that night he thanked God for a beautiful day and for the wonderful world he had made. He finished his prayer "I thank you, God, that I can always depend on you, because Daddy says You are always the same, yesterday, today and for ever".

(Faithfulness of God: Hebrews ch. 13 v. 8; James ch. 1 v. 17b)

Free air today, free petrol tomorrow

Boys and girls if you watch the T.V. or read the newspapers you will know this is the age of advertisements. All kinds of things are being advertised today with all kinds of slogans and special offers to entice people to buy. I remember hearing once about a garage which had a big notice which said, 'Free Air Today, Free Petrol tomorrow'.

One day a motorist drove in and got air in his tyres and when he was leaving he said, "I'll be back for the free petrol tomorrow". Sure enough the next day he arrived at the garage and asked for four gallons of free petrol.

He said, "I was here yesterday and got the free air". The attendant said, "You haven't read the notice correctly. It says 'Free air today - free petrol tomorrow'. This is today and it's only free air now". "Oh, I see", said the motorist, "tomorrow never comes".

In one sense it is true. Tomorrow never comes - that's why we should not leave off till tomorrow what we can do today.

The Bible says:

"Today, if you will hear God's voice - harden not your heart".

"Give yourselves this day to the Lord".

"Now is the day of salvation".

All God's gifts and blessing are here for us today and if we are wise we will accept them now - not tomorrow but today.

(Decision: 2 Corinthians ch. 6 v. 2; Hebrews ch. 3 v. 15)

Jimmy hit me back

One day on the way home from school wee Johnny and his friend Jimmy began to argue about something that was of no importance at all. You know how boys and girls can quarrel sometimes about things that don't really matter. Well that's what happened to Johnny and Jimmy.

It all began with quite a friendly argument; then they started to get annoyed with each other; before long they had lost their tempers. Then Johnny hit Jimmy and of course Jimmy hit him back. So they began to fight. Just when they were well started who should come along the road but Johnny's Mammy. "Tut, tut", she said, "Imagine two friends like you fighting like that! How did it start?"

"How did it start?" repeated Johnny, "It all started when Jimmy hit me back". Well, of course, in one sense, that was right enough, because you couldn't have an argument or you couldn't have a fight if one of the people refused to quarrel. Indeed it is very hard to refuse to quarrel, yet that is what every follower of Jesus is expected to do and commanded to do. "If any man strike you on the right cheek turn to him the other also". Don't hit back, don't fight back. Maybe you think that would be silly, but that's just what Jesus did himself. Although he was tormented and teased by all sorts of people, beaten, insulted, spat upon and even put to death on the cross, He never, never retaliated or hit back. Yet it was Jesus, and not his enemies, who came out victorious. Next time you are tempted to lose your temper with someone or to try to get your own back, will you remember the example of Jesus and His commandment? "If any man strike you on the right cheek, turn to him the other also".

(Forgiveness: Matthew ch. 5 v. 39)

Understandest thou what thou readest?

Do you understand what you are reading? This question was put by Philip to an Ethiopian who was sitting one day in his chariot at the roadside, reading the book of the Prophet Isaiah. There were not many books in those days and there weren't many people who could read. There are still a big number of boys and girls in this country who leave school without being able to read.

I'm sure, boys and girls, that you can all read. It's very important to be able to read and it's also very important to understand what you read.

One Sunday in wee Johnny's class in Sunday School the lesson was about the flight of Mary, Joseph and the Baby Jesus into Egypt. You remember why they went into Egypt - it was to save the life of the Baby Jesus after Herod had decreed the death of all the children under 2 years of age in Bethlehem. Johnny's teacher read the story and then she asked all the class to draw a picture of it and bring it next Sunday. One little boy drew a most elaborate picture. He drew Joseph and Mary with the baby in her arms, trudging along the dusty road. Behind them he drew a strange looking insect, like a big spider. "What's that?" said the teacher. "That's the flea", said the boy. "Didn't the angel tell Joseph to take Mary and the baby and 'flea' into Egypt?" Now that wee boy should have known the difference between flea and flee. He wouldn't have made that silly mistake if he had understood what he was reading.

What kind of a picture do you think wee Johnny drew? Well he thought that "the flight" into Egypt was done in an aeroplane. So he drew a big plane up in the sky with Mary, Joseph and the Baby Jesus as passengers. Up at the front of the plane was a figure and wee Johnny said to the teacher, "That is 'Pontius the Pilate'". Now I'm sure all you boys and girls know that the pilot who flies an aeroplane spells his name differently from the man who was the judge of Jesus before his crucifixion. And even the youngest boy or girl knows there were no aeroplanes in the days of Jesus. You see now how important it is to understand what you read.

When Philip explained to the Ethiopian the meaning of what he was reading, he became a Christian, a follower of Jesus. The wonderful thing about the Bible is that you don't need to be very old or very clever to enjoy it and to be blessed by its stories.

So learn, even when you are young, to understand what you read and never forget that the best book to read is the Bible.

(Bible / Christmas: Matthew ch. 2 v. 13; Acts ch. 8 v. 30)

Family heirloom

In wee Johnny's house there was a very beautiful glass ornament. It had been handed down from generation to generation. Johnny's Mammy was very proud of it. Often she told people the story behind it, how it had belonged to her great-grandmother and how carefully it had been passed on, first to her grandmother, then her mother and then to her. As long as wee Johnny could remember it had stood in the centre of the drawing room mantelpiece. One day when he had the house to himself he went into the drawing room and stood looking at the ornament. He wondered for a long time if he dare touch it. Then he pulled over a chair and climbed up and reached out his hand. With a firm grip he caught the ornament and was just about to climb down when the chair slipped, Johnny slipped and the ornament slipped and broke into a hundred pieces.

Poor Johnny! He was very silent all evening and no one knew his secret until bedtime. When he was settled in bed he said to his Mammy. "You know that precious ornament, the one that was handed down from generation to generation?" "Yes", said his Mammy, "what about it?" "Well", said Johnny, "this generation has dropped it".

You know boys and girls many beautiful things have been handed down to us from generation to generation. We must be careful to hold on to them firmly and not let them drop. Things like the Bible, Sunday, the Church and the Christian faith itself. Many of these things were bought for us by men who gave their lives for them. We must learn to value and respect them. May we never have to make the sad confession Johnny had to make - this generation has dropped it.

(Heritage: Titus ch. 1 v. 9; 2 Timothy ch. 1 vs. 13, 14)

Johnny's new house

Did I ever tell you about the time wee Johnny moved to a new house? Nobody had lived in it for some time and there was a lot of work to do both in the house and in the garden. Every day when he came home from school Johnny and his Daddy worked hard in the garden.

They cut grass and hedges and they dug over all the flower beds and planted bulbs and shrubs. They had to work really hard, but in the summer when the flowers began to bloom and the lawn was nicely cut it looked beautiful.

One day some friends of the family called to see the new house. After tea they went out into the garden and it was a lovely day. They admired the neat lawn and the lovely flowers. Then one of them said to Johnny, "Isn't it wonderful what God can do in a garden?" Wee Johnny thought of all the days he and his Daddy had spent at it and how hard they had worked. Then he answered, "No doubt God can do wonderful things in a garden but you should have seen it when God had it to himself".

That was Johnny's way of saying he had helped God to make the garden beautiful. There are lots of things God needs our help to do. We give thanks for the food and fruit of the earth and we also give thanks for all the different people who have helped God to bring His gifts to us. And if we are really grateful we will show our gratitude by offering God the service of our lives.

(Gratitude: Romans ch. 12 v. 1)

Lying lips

One day in Sunday School the lesson set was shorter than usual and wee Johnny's class was finished before the time; so the teacher decided to have a competition. She gave all the boys a piece of paper and a pencil and this was the idea. The teacher would give them the start of a text from the Bible and they were to finish the text and write the name of the book in which it was found. There were six texts altogether. I wonder how many you would have got right.

1. "I will life up mine eyes . . ." That was a very easy one, and all the boys got it right. "I will life up mine eyes unto the hills from whence cometh my help". And it comes from the Psalms.

2. "Bring forth the best robe . . . " That was easy to finish, but not quite so easy to say which book it was in. "Bring forth the best robe and put it on Him, put a ring on His hand and shoes on His feet" comes from the story of the Prodigal Son and is found only in Luke's Gospel.

3. "Remember now . . ." That is finished by "Remember now thy creator in the days of thy youth" in the book of Ecclesiastes.

4. "In the beginning God . . ." That's the first verse in the Bible in the book of Genesis "In the beginning God created the heaven and the earth".

5. "All things work together for good . . ." Not many of the boys knew where this verse came from - from the Epistle to the Romans. "All things work together for good to them that love God".

6. The last verse was the greatest puzzle of all. None of the boys were able to finish it correctly although wee Johnny made a shot at it, and he guessed that it came from the book

of Proverbs. But he wasn't so good at guessing how it finished.

The verse began "Lying lips are abomination to the Lord but . . ." Johnny wrote "Lying lips are abomination to the Lord but a very present help in time of trouble". You know there are some people and they act as if Johnny's answer was correct. They get into trouble about something, maybe at school or at home and they think perhaps they can get out of it by telling a lie. But that never works. For you see, whenever the truth comes to light, as it always does you find yourself in greater trouble than ever. It's always far better to stick to the truth and the teaching of the book of Proverbs. "Lying lips are abomination to the Lord, but they that deal truly are His delight".

(Telling lies: Proverbs ch. 12 v. 22)

O for a thousand tongues

When I am on holiday and go to a church as a visitor I like to look at the hymns on the board before the service to see what we are going to sing. I always look particularly at the closing hymn and try to guess from it what the minister is going to preach about.

Today I want to ask you a riddle about a hymn. I'm sure you are all good at riddles - well listen carefully. If wee Johnny fell into a barrel of ice cream what hymn would he sing?

You might guess "From Greenland's Icy Mountains", but you wouldn't be right. You might guess "Rescue the Perishing" but you still wouldn't be right! Will I tell you the answer? It's the hymn "O for a thousand tongues". You see Johnny is very fond of ice cream and one wee tongue wouldn't be much use in a barrel of it. "O for a thousand tongues". These words were written by one of the greatest hymn writers of all time - Charles Wesley. But of course he wasn't thinking about wee Johnny or ice cream when he wrote this hymn. What was he thinking about?

He was thinking of all the wonder of the love of Jesus. "O for a thousand tongues to sing my great Redeemer's praise". We can never thank God enough for all His goodness to us. All we have and all we are we owe to Him. He is the giver of every good and perfect gift. The best of all His gifts to us is Jesus Christ, His Son.

When Charles Wesley thought of Him he wrote "O for a thousand tongues to sing my great Redeemer's praise".

(God's love: 2 Corinthians ch. 9 v. 15)

Johnny's waistcoat

Johnny got the present of a smart new waistcoat. It had two pockets and a long row of buttons. He tried it on and went over to the mirror to look at himself and he saw at once there was something wrong. The waistcoat was all twisted and no matter how he tugged and pulled at it, he couldn't get it straight. Then he looked at it more closely and he discovered that there was a button too many on it at the top.

So he went to his Daddy. "Look Daddy", he said, "this waistcoat's all wrong. There's an extra button on it at the top and it won't sit straight". So his Daddy looked at it. "Right enough", he said, "there is a button too many on it at the top. But look down", he added, "you'll see that there's a button hole too many at the bottom".

"You see", said his Daddy, as he opened it and started to button it correctly, "if you don't start right, you can't finish right".

It was a lesson Johnny will never forget and one which we should all learn in life. "If you don't start right, you can't finish right". That's true of many things but it is especially true of life itself. There are lots of people in the world and they are all twisted and mixed up because they haven't started in the right place. They will never be right until they go back to the beginning and start all over again. Begin with Jesus because without Him you will never make much of life, no matter how hard you try. Ask Jesus for His forgiveness, for His guidance and His help to keep you straight and true to the end of the journey.

(New birth: John ch. 3 v. 3)

Life story of a turkey

On the week before Christmas the teacher in wee Johnny's class at school asked the boys and girls to write a composition. What do you think the subject was? It was "The story of my life - by a turkey".

I'm sure you would like to hear what wee Johnny wrote. Well, here it is:

"I was hatched out of a great big egg. I do not remember my mother. Maybe she died when I was very young, because I was brought up by a hen on a farm. I had two brothers and three sisters so there were six in our family counting me. My foster mother was very good to me. Every night we slept under her wings until we grew too big to fit in. Then we had to learn to sleep on a perch. The farmer's wife was very kind. I was fed like a king and when it was wet I was kept in the house. I grew very quickly and the farmer's wife used to catch me every now and then to feel how fat I was. Then one morning just before Christmas, the strangest thing happened. The farmer came and caught me and pulled my neck, and I was dead for the rest of my life".

That was Johnny's composition and wasn't that a funny sentence to finish with - "I was dead for the rest of my life". Unfortunately that is sometimes true for men and women. The Bible tells us "In Him was life" and Jesus said, "I am come that they might have life". To be without Jesus is to be dead. Because Adam sinned, we are separated from God and because God is the source of all life, to be separated from Him is to die. If we are to have the life that Jesus came to give us then we have to open our hearts to Him and let Him come and live with us.

(Christmas: John ch. 10 v. 10)

Did you weigh Johnny?

One Saturday wee Johnny was hanging about the house with nothing to do. So his Mammy wrote out a list of things she wanted from the shop - tea, sugar, butter, cheese, a pot of marmalade and 2 pounds of apples. She gave the list to Johnny and sent him to the shop. When he got back his Mammy was busy so she didn't unpack the groceries until Johnny was in bed. Everything was in order except the apples. She had been charged for 2 pounds but when she weighed them there was only 1 1/2 pounds. She was surprised that the shop owner would give her short weight. So next time she was in the shop she mentioned it to him. The shopman said, "I don't think I made a mistake but tell me when you weighed the apples did you weigh Johnny too?" "You know", said his Mammy, "I never thought of that".

That day when Johnny came home from school his Mammy put him on the scales. I don't mean she weighed him in stones and pounds, but as the Bible says, "He was weighed in the balance and found wanting". He told his Mammy he had eaten some apples on his way home. "I thought no one would have noticed", he added. "Well", said his Mammy, "it's not the value of the apples, but you should never take anything without asking. I never thought of you eating them and I almost accused the shopkeeper of giving me short weight".

"I'm sorry", said Johnny, "I'll not do it again". And there and then he made up his mind to be frank about everything and when he made a mistake he would admit it, so that no one else would be wrongly blamed.

(Honesty: Daniel ch. 5 v. 27)

School Report

I wonder if any of the boys and girls at church today were up early yesterday morning? Why do I ask? Because yesterday morning the results of the Eleven Plus Test were to arrive by post and it was an anxious day for many boys and girls. One day wee Johnny got up early because he thought his school report would be arriving. Sure enough, when the postman left the letters Johnny recognised one of them - it was his school report. He rushed upstairs to his Daddy and he said, "It's here today". "What is?" asked his Daddy. "My school report", answered Johnny. So he watched as his Daddy opened the letter and studied his face as he read it. This is what he read: English - Good; Arithmetic - Fair; French - Poor; History - Very Poor. Then suddenly his face grew brighter and he began to smile because the headmaster's report said, "Johnny is the most cheerful and the most honourable boy in the school".

"There son", he said, as he reached it to Johnny, "It's an excellent report". As Johnny slipped out of the room his Daddy said to his Mammy, "I would like Johnny to be clever, but if I had to choose between cleverness and goodness, I would choose goodness every time".

Boys and girls we can't all be clever but we can all be good. Some years ago there was a boy at a very famous English school. He often failed his exams and was usually the bottom of his class. His teachers thought he would make little of his life. His name was Winston Churchill and he became one of the greatest Prime Ministers of Britain. The lesson for all of us is to do our best and use all the gifts God has given us. If your report is not too good don't lose heart or give up hope. Remember Winston Churchill and what wee Johnny's Daddy said, "If I had to choose between goodness and cleverness I'd choose goodness every time".

(Goodness)

SCHOOL
REPORT

Build a garage or get married

One time wee Johnny's older sister Mary fell in love and there was great excitement in the house. Nearly every night her boyfriend called to take her out. Although he hadn't much money he had bought a car. It was an old car and when it was a wet night, or a frosty night, it was hard to start the next morning.

Mary's boyfriend knew that the only answer to this was to build a garage. He wanted to get married to Mary and he wanted to build a garage but he couldn't do both for he hadn't enough money. He thought about it seriously and asked a few of his friends. Some of them said, "Build a garage", and others said, "Get married".

Then one night he asked wee Johnny and he got a quick and definite reply. "You should build the garage", said Johnny, "because you can always back out of it".

You see Johnny knew that when you get married you can't back out of it - because marriage is for life. That is just the way we are bound to Jesus - it is a service for life. There are a great many organisations you can join and you can leave them whenever you like. But the service of Jesus isn't like that. When we decide to follow Him we can't back out of it. That was why Jesus said, "Whosoever putteth his hand to the plough and looketh back is not fit for the Kingdom of God".

You see just as Jesus gave all that He had for us so He wants us to give Him all we have, not only now, but always. This is the great secret of joy and happiness in life, to serve and follow Jesus to the end.

(Marriage; Faithfulness: Luke ch. 9 v. 62)

Sins of omission

One day in school when the roll had been called wee Johnny held up his hand and said, "Please Miss, would you punish me for something I didn't do?" "Oh no Johnny", answered the teacher, "that wouldn't be fair. I wouldn't punish anyone for something they didn't do". "I'm very glad to hear that", said Johnny, "for I didn't do my homework".

Of course Johnny had deceived the teacher. If he had asked, "Would you punish me for something I ought to have done and didn't do?", I'm sure the answer would have been different. That's what we call a sin of omission - omitting to do something we ought to do. It's a good thing to remember there are sins like that. Many of the people who were condemned by Jesus were condemned not for what they did, but for what they didn't do.

You remember the story of the Good Samaritan? How the Priest and the Levite saw the wounded man and they passed by without helping - on the other side. That was a sin of omission. You remember the parable of the talents and the man who hid his talent in the ground instead of using it? That was a sin of omission.

You remember the rich man who refused to help the poor beggar? That was a sin of omission.

All through the New Testament you come across stories of people who were condemned by Jesus not for what they did but for what they failed to do.

Will you remember that the next time you have a bag of sweets which you know you ought to share but which you want to eat yourself. Remember it when you have the chance of being kind and helpful to someone in need. If there is any good thing you ought to have done and didn't do, ask God to forgive you and to help you not to make the same mistake again.

(Sins of omission; The Good Samaritan: James ch. 4 v. 17)

The funniest thing I have never seen

One day in school the teacher asked the class to write a composition. I'm sure you would never guess what they were to write about. The subject was "The funniest thing I have ever seen". When wee Johnny heard the subject he thought for a moment that he might write about the teacher, but he decided, very wisely, that she mightn't see the joke, so he changed his mind. It wasn't long before all the class were writing furiously, all except Johnny. He had seen so many funny things that he didn't know which of them to write about. At last he took up his pen and wrote at the top of the page "The funniest thing I have ever seen".

He wrote very slowly and carefully and he was finished long before anyone else in the class. Would you like to hear what he wrote? It didn't take long to write and it takes even less time to read. It has only one sentence - "The funniest thing I have ever seen was too funny for words".

I don't know what the teacher thought of that, but I do know that Johnny was copying a good example. Let me explain.

Another very famous person and famous writer couldn't find words to express what he wanted to write. He wasn't writing about the funniest thing he had ever seen, but about the greatest gift he had ever received.

His name was Paul and the greatest gift was Jesus Christ. Even Paul, who wrote a big part of the New Testament didn't know what to say about Jesus. He wrote in his letter to the people of Corinth, "Thanks be unto God for His unspeakable gift". It was too wonderful for words - an unspeakable gift.

That's what Jesus is to all who have opened their hearts to Him. No words can express the wonder of God's love but if we cannot say it in words we can say it by deeds.

We can say thanks for the greatest gift we have ever received, by loving God and by loving our neighbour as ourselves.

(God's love: Matthew ch. 5 v. 16; 2 Corinthians ch. 9 v. 15)

Johnny and the custard

I'm sorry to have to tell you that Johnny was a bad boy during the week. This is how it happened. One day when he came home from school his Mammy was baking in the kitchen. She had made scones and buns and best of all she had made a dish of custard and Johnny just loved custard.

When she had everything finished she said she had to go out and she told Johnny to start his school lessons and not to touch any of the things she had made. Johnny started his lessons but then he thought about the custard and he went and looked at it but said, "No, no, I was told not to touch anything", so he went back to his lessons. He just couldn't forget that dish of custard, so he decided to get a spoon just to taste it. He took one spoonful and it was so delicious he took another and another, and before he realised what he had done the custard was half way down the dish. Poor Johnny, what would his Mammy say? Just then he noticed the cat and he hit on the idea of blaming the cat. So he caught the cat and pushed her nose into the dish to make his story look better. When his mother came back she noticed the dish of custard. "Did you touch the custard Johnny?" she asked. "No", came the answer and then Johnny said, "Look Mammy! Look at the cat! See the custard on her face". "Well", said his Mammy, "Just look at her but it's the first time I heard of a cat eating custard with a spoon". Poor Johnny he had forgotten to wash the spoon. He wasn't just as clever as he thought because his sin had found him out. It was a sad and sorry little boy who got into Johnny's bed that night.

(Honesty: Numbers ch. 32 v. 23)

Go, tell

In wee Johnny's school there is a Debating Society and one of the rules is that every boy in turn has to make a speech. The first time Johnny got up to speak he forgot what he was going to say. "Do any of you know what I am going to talk about?" he asked and there was a loud "No" from all the boys and girls in the class. "Well, neither do I", said Johnny, and sat down.

The next time it was Johnny's turn the same thing happened; he forgot what he was going to say. "Do any of you know what I am going to talk about?" he asked. The boys and girls were not going to be caught again so they shouted "Yes". "Well", said Johnny, "if you all know I don't need to tell you", and he sat down. The third time it was Johnny's turn he forgot again. "Do any of you know what I am going to talk about?" This time some of the class shouted "Yes" and some of them shouted "No". "Well", said Johnny, "in that case, those who know can tell those who don't know". And that was the end of Johnny's speech.

That, of course, is not the way a Debating Society is supposed to work, but strange as it may seem, it is the very way Jesus used for building the Kingdom of God. Those who know can tell those who don't know. If we have found Jesus for ourselves it is our duty to tell others who do not know Him. We do that in the church by sending missionaries to preach about Jesus in other lands. But we can all do it at home in a very simple way. We can tell others about Jesus by the way we live. If we have the spirit of Jesus in our hearts then we will be kind, unselfish and honourable. In that way we can bear witness to our faith. "Go ye into all the world and preach the gospel" is the command of Christ, and if we are to keep that command we who know Jesus must tell those who don't.

(Evangelism: Mark ch. 16 v. 15)

Mother's Day

One Sunday in Sunday School the lesson was on happiness - not only how to be happy ourselves but how to make others happy too. The teacher told the boys and girls how much of the life of Jesus was spent bringing gladness to the hearts of other people. The teacher said, "How many of you did anything last week to make others happy?"

One girl told how her Mammy had a cold and how she had helped in the house. One boy told how he had invited one of his friends to his home and let him ride on his new bicycle. Another girl told how she had bought two bars of chocolate with her pocket money and had given her friend one of them. While all this was going on wee Johnny was puzzling in his mind about what on earth he had done to make others happy and at last he thought of something. The teacher said, "What about you Johnny?" So Johnny said, "Yesterday I went to spend the day in the country with my friend JImmy. We had a great day. We slid down the hay in the shed, we kicked football on the lawn, we played firemen and lit a fire in the yard and put it out with buckets of water".

"Well", said the teacher, "I don't see how that made anyone happy except you yourself". "Oh it did", said Johnny, "it made Jimmy's Mammy happy because she was so pleased when I said it was time to go home".

Well now, I hope there is one person who will be very happy when you go home today. Guess who? Your Mammy. This is Mother's Day and I want all of you to try very hard to make your mother happy today and every day. You can do that by helping in the house, by being obedient and, above all, by being grateful for all the love and care which you receive from the best friend you will ever have - your mother.

Making music

How many of the boys and girls have heard of Fritz Kreisler? He was one of the world's most famous violinists. He was born in 1875 and when he was a wee boy he was a great musician.

The story is told that, one day, he was walking down the street when he heard the sound of a violin with a tone and beauty such as he had never heard before. The music was coming from the shop of a violin maker and Kreisler went in and asked if he could buy the instrument which he had just heard being played. The violin maker said he was sorry but he could not sell it. It had just been bought by a man who could not play at all, but who collected violins.

So Kreisler got his name and address and went to see him to ask if he would sell the violin. The collector refused to sell it but said, "Perhaps you would like to play a tune on it". Kreisler picked it up and began to play, and when he had finished the collector turned to him with tears in his eyes. "Take it", he said, "take it for nothing. It should not belong to me, it should belong to you. Take it and waken its music that all may hear".

You see that violin in the hands of the collector was dumb, but in the hands of the master it produced the most wonderful music in the world.

Our lives are just like that. If we want them to produce music of beauty and joy we must put them into the hands of the Master. That is why Christ calls us and it is only when we open our hearts to Him and are filled with the Spirit that we can live our lives to the glory of God and bring happiness to the hearts of others.

(Fulfilment)

A
D

Sit still and keep quiet

There has been great activity in wee Johnny's house recently because his baby sister is learning to walk and talk. Everyone is helping her to walk and teaching her to say wee words. Johnny just loves to look after her and there is nothing he likes better than to have her all to himself. Every day when he comes in from school his first question is "Where's the baby?" One day when Johnny came home from school his Mammy was very busy in the kitchen, baking and cooking, because she was having visitors for tea. Johnny said, "Can I play with the baby? I'll look after her for you and let you get on with your work". Nothing seemed to go right. The baby fell and bumped her head and she started to cry. Johnny was jumping around trying to amuse her but she kept on crying.

At last Johnny's Mammy came in and put the baby in the pram and told Johnny "to sit down and keep quiet". Poor Johnny, he was doing his best but it was one of those days when everything went wrong. That night when the visitors had gone home and Johnny was going to bed, his Mammy came in to say good-night. Johnny said, "Mammy, when I was a baby did everybody try to teach me to walk and talk?" "Indeed, yes", said his Mammy. Johnny said "Isn't it funny the trouble we go to teaching babies to walk and talk and then when they are a bit older, like me, we start telling them to sit still and keep quiet".

They both laughed and then his Mammy read Johnny two verses from the Bible. The first verse from the Psalms. "Be still and know that I am God".

The second one from Ecclesiastes - "To everything there is a season and a time to every purpose under the heaven - a time to keep silence and a time to speak".

Take these two texts for today.

(Timing: Psalm 46 v. 10 Ecclesiastes ch. 3 vs. 1, 7b)

Johnny late for church

One Sunday in wee Johnny's house everyone slept in, including Johnny himself. His Daddy said, "We couldn't be in time for church today", and he decided to just lie in. But Johnny had different ideas. "I haven't missed church this year yet and I'm going to try to be in time". He jumped up and gave himself a quick wash and got dressed. When he came down his Mammy had his breakfast ready and he ate it as quickly as he could. He got his hymn book and offering and got his bicycle ready. "Take your time now Johnny. It doesn't matter if you are a wee bit late". Johnny was away in a flash and cycling as hard as he could.

"I might be a wee bit late", Johnny thought, "but I'll not be too bad". When he got to the church there was nobody outside, and he could hear the people singing inside. He slipped into his seat and they were just finishing the last verse of the hymn. And then guess what happened? Johnny sat down but everybody else stayed standing. Then he could hardly believe his ears when he heard the minister pronouncing the benediction.

You know what had happened? He had forgotten to put his watch forward 1 hour, so instead of being a few minutes late, he was 1 hour late. Everybody smiled at Johnny and thought it was the shortest service he had ever been at but at least he was there and he still hasn't missed church this year yet.

You know sometimes it's hard to remember whether to put the clock forwards an hour or back an hour. Well a way to help you remember which way to turn your clock is the phrase "Spring Forward: Fall Back". ("Fall" is what Americans call Autumn). God always calls us to spring forward in his service and to fall back from all evil.

(Changing the clock)

Johnny's new bicycle

Did you ever hear about the time wee Johnny got a new bicycle? Although he couldn't ride a bicycle, he wanted one more than anything else. On the morning of his birthday, when he came downstairs, there sitting in the hall was a new bicycle. It was perfect and just the very thing Johnny had dreamed of. For many days he had to get his Mammy or Daddy to go with him to teach him to ride. At last the great day came when he was able to ride on his own. Of course he wasn't very good at first and he had 2 or 3 falls. Then one day, he went out on to the road and all went well because there was very little traffic. Suddenly, as he came round a corner, he saw a man walking along the side of the road. As he was about to pass him the man stepped out and Johnny was not able to put on his brakes in time and knocked him down. He shouted at Johnny, "Can you not ring your bell?" "Oh yes", said Johnny, "I can ring my bell O.k. but I'm not very good at riding the bicycle". The man laughed and said to Johnny, "Be more careful next time you go cycling".

You know, boys and girls, there are lots of people in the world who can ring the bell, but are not very good at riding the bicycle. People who can talk a great deal and make plenty of noise, but when it comes to doing something they are not very good at that. There are people who make a great song about their religion but when it comes to being kind, unselfish and honest they make a poor effort at that. It is a good thing to be able and ready to bear witness to your faith but it is a far, far better thing to let your life speak for itself. Learn first to follow in the footsteps of Jesus and to live like Him every day. That's the most important thing and when you have learned to do that, then you can bear witness with your words.

Remember it is more important to be able to ride the bicycle than to ring the bell.

(Doers of the Word: 1 Corinthians ch. 4 v. 20)

Picture of the fall

One day in wee Johnny's class in Sunday School the lesson was on the fall and Genesis chapter 3 was the passage of scripture. The teacher read the story from the bible and explained the story of the fall as best she could. Then she said, "Now I want you all to draw a picture of the fall". I need hardly tell you that there were some wonderful productions. There were all kinds of pictures of Adam and Eve, the serpent, the Tree of Knowledge, the cherubims and the flaming sword. Wee Johnny had drawn a very elaborate picture. In the background he had a garden with flowers, trees and a hedge all round it. At the front there was a big iron gate leading on to a big wide road. Coming out of the gate on to the road was a big Rolls Royce car. In the back of the car sat Adam and Eve and in front there was a chauffeur with his uniform on. When the teacher looked at it she asked Johnny to explain it and he said, "That's Adam and Eve being driven from the garden".

Of course, Johnny had missed the meaning of the story, that by the fall, Adam and Eve sinned against God and had to leave the perfect happiness of the Garden of Eden. They were not driven out in a Rolls Royce as Johnny had pictured them. They were driven out in sorrow, shame and disgrace. But worst of all, by their sin, they cut themselves off from the friendship of God. But God was not content to leave His children like that so in the fullness of time He sent His son, Jesus. By giving His life on the cross Jesus paid the price of man's sin and opened the way for us to come back to God's friendship. That's what it means when it tells us in the Bible "As in Adam all die, even so in Christ shall all be made alive". What we could not do, God in His mercy has done for us through Christ.

(The Fall: Genesis ch. 3; 1 Corinthians ch. 15 v. 22)

29th February ...the extra day

Last Tuesday was the 29th February and in wee Johnny's class at school the teacher asked them to write a composition entitled "The 29th February". I'm sure you would like to hear what wee Johnny wrote - well here it is.

"The month of February is the shortest month of the year. It has only 28 days except in a leap year when it has an extra day. There is a leap year every 4 years and it is always a dangerous time for boys - because in a leap year girls can ask boys to marry them. People who are born on the 29th February are very unfortunate because they only have a birthday every four years. The reason why there are leap years is that the earth goes round the sun, not in 365 days, but in 3651/4 days. If nobody bothered about the extra 1/4 day the earth and the sun would soon get out of step. So instead of adding on 1/4 of a day every year, we add on one whole day every four years. This is on the 29th of February. This extra day is like a Sunday - because it is put in to keep everything right".

Isn't that a very good composition for wee Johnny to write. I think that's a lovely sentence at the end "This extra day is like a Sunday - because it is put in to keep everything right".

You know why we go to Sunday School and Church on Sunday? We go to worship God and to learn about Jesus. When we do that it helps to keep us right for the rest of the week.

A Sunday well spent brings a week of content
And joy for the cares of tomorrow
But a Sunday profaned - whatever be gained
Is a certain forerunner of sorrow.

(Sunday; February 29th)

Buckets and baskets

Boys and girls, there is an old story of a king who wanted to find a faithful servant and soon the news spread throughout his kingdom. Many of his subjects came to offer their services and out of them all the King chose two. He decided to test them himself and he did it in a very curious way. He gave each of them a bucket, a basket and a rope and he sent them to a well. He told them that, bucket by bucket, they were to empty the well of water and to pour each bucketful into their basket. And so they began.

Bucket after bucket was lifted out and poured into the baskets and, of course, it only trickled away and left the baskets as empty as ever. Before long one of the men got tired. "This is a fool's job", he said, "The water only runs away". And he gave up. The other man said, "This is the task the King asked me to do and no matter how silly it may seem, I will keep at it". He went on lowering his bucket into the well, lifting it up and pouring the water into the basket. Through time he came to the bottom of the well and as he peered down his eye caught the glitter of something shining in the mud. It was a precious diamond ring. "Ah", he said, "I see now why the King made us pour the water through the basket - to find the ring". The King said to him, "You are the man I can trust. You trusted me even when you did not understand my ways". And he gave him a high position in his kingdom.

There is a lesson in that story for every boy and girl. Sometimes you are asked by your parents to do things you do not understand, but remember your parents love you and they are wise and you must learn to trust and obey them and do what they ask. There is a lesson here for us all for we are all children - the children of God. Sometimes we do not under stand the ways and the plans of God but we must remember that God loves us and knows what is best for us.

Whatever He asks we must do without question. As the old hymn says:-

"Trust and obey,
For there's no other way
To be happy in Jesus
But to trust and obey".

(Trust, Obedience: Proverbs ch. 3 v. 5)

James Garfield and his mother

Back in 1831 a baby boy was born in America and his name was James Garfield. His parents were very poor and they lived in the country in a tiny log cabin. When James grew up he worked hard and by perseverance he made his way up until at last he was elected President of the United States. Before he was installed as President he wrote to his mother and asked her to come with him to Washington. She wrote back and said that she would feel out of place with all those important people. "I will just stay at home and pray for you", she said. Her son wrote back and said, "I will not go without you".

So the old lady travelled to Washington and stayed in the hotel with her son. When the time for the great ceremony came she went out linked arm and arm with her son. There was a huge crowd and on the platform sat famous people from all over the country.

Together Garfield and his mother climbed on to the platform and in front of all the people he gave his mother his chair, the seat of honour provided for himself. After he had take the oath to be faithful to his office, he turned and put his arms round his mother and kissed her.

Why did he do that? Because he knew how much his mother had done for him and how much he owed to her. Although we may never rise to such heights as James Garfield, nobody has done more for us than our mothers. The debt we owe is more than we can ever repay. Boys and girls I hope you will all remember that not only today, on Mother's Day but every day. Do your best to show a little love and gratitude for all that has been done for you.

(Mother's Day: Exodus ch. 20 v. 12)

This little card

One day last week Johnny got money from his Mammy to buy Christmas cards to send to his friends. He wanted to buy seven altogether, six for his chums at school and one very special one for a wee girl who lived near him. He picked a nice little card with a nice picture - here it is. It has a picture of a little girl sitting on a cloud in the sky knitting a great big Christmas stocking. This is not an ordinary wee girl because she has wings like an angel and a halo over her head. Johnny thought it was a very suitable card because he thought his little girl friend was really angelic. But he never posted it because he hadn't looked inside it until he got home. The card had a verse inside which read "This little card is just to say, a Christmas gift is on its way". Johnny didn't send the card because he had no intention of sending a gift.

I know someone else who once sent a message like that with the promise of a present but it was followed by the best Christmas gift of all. "Unto you a child is born, unto you a Son is given and His name shall be called Wonderful, Counsellor, The Mighty God, The Everlasting Father, The Prince of Peace". This is the promise of the first and best of all Christmas gifts. It was written many years before Jesus was born by the prophet Isaiah and, of course, it was fulfilled at the first Christmas at Bethlehem.

Do you remember what Paul wrote about the coming of Jesus - "Thanks be unto God for His unspeakable gift". I hope, amid all the excitement and joy of Christmas, you will not forget to be grateful to God for His unspeakable gift and remember too that the best way to show your gratitude is by giving your life to Him.

(Christmas: Romans ch 8 v. 32; 2 Corinthians ch. 9 v. 15)

Granny's Finals

Last week was a very difficult one for wee Johnny and I'll tell you why. His big sister was home from University and she was studying very hard for her exams. These were the last exams she would ever sit (she hoped!) and they were called her "Finals". And wee Johnny had to tiptoe around the house, just in case he disturbed her. So, he found it a very long week.

However, it was all forgotten at the weekend when Johnny went to stay with his Granny. What made it even better, was that Johnny was allowed to bring his little friend Jimmy with him. On Saturday morning when they were running around the house making a bit of noise, Johnny noticed that his Granny was sitting reading her Bible.

"Shush!" said Johnny, "We better be quiet. Granny's swotting for her finals".

I don't think for one moment Johnny understood what he was saying but there is a lot of truth in it. For one thing there is the truth of the final exam which we all have to face. Jesus explained it in the parable of the last judgment (Matt. 25, 31-46).

Another truth is that it is only in the Bible that we learn how to pass this examination. It's not a matter of what we know or what we say but of what we do. According to Jesus this is how God divides the sheep from the goats, the good from the bad. This is the greatest test of all and whether we pass or fail depends on the love in our hearts. With love we will win a wonderful prize. Without love we will fail and be punished.

That is why Jesus told us to love God and to love our neighbour.

(The Last Judgment: Matthew ch. 25, vs. 31-46)

God
is
Love
HOLY
BIBLE

'Soldiers are we'

One day wee Johnny got out of the wrong side of the bed. To begin with he hadn't his lessons done for school. He had intended to get up early and do them in the morning but he slept in and when he discovered he was late he lost his temper. He pulled on his clothes without washing his face or doing his teeth.

When he came downstairs he said he didn't want any breakfast. "Don't be silly", said his Mammy, "Go and dress yourself properly and then come and take your breakfast". "I don't want any breakfast", sulked Johnny. To cut a long story short it was a very untidy boy, with an empty tummy and a bad temper who set off for school. It was a bad start and it didn't get any better as the day went on. He fell out with his school friends and disagreed with his teacher and finished up by being kept in.

When he came home, Johnny threw his bag down and shouted, "I hate old school, I wish I could run away and join the army". "Don't be silly", said his Mammy, "You are far too young". "Well I wouldn't tell them my right age", said Johnny. "You might add a few years to your age but you couldn't add a few inches to your height", said his Mammy, "You are too small".

"Well", said Johnny, "I'd join the army down South! They would take me in to it because there they are always singing 'Soldiers are wee'". His Mammy laughed and when she explained what "Soldiers are we" really meant, Johnny saw the joke and laughed himself. Then he said he was sorry for being bad tempered and when he had tidied himself and had a good tea, he started into his lessons.

That night when he was going to bed his Mammy came and tucked him in. "You know Johnny", she said, "If you really want to be a soldier, you don't need to wait until you leave school and grow up. Many years ago Paul wrote to his young friend Timothy and said - 'Be a good soldier of Jesus Christ'".

That night before he went to sleep Johnny volunteered, and offered his life to the service of Christ.

*(Following Jesus:
2 Timothy
ch. 2, v. 3)*

Appendix

The next 5 children's addresses were given in 1957 and they introduced "The Wee Johnny Club" in Trinity Presbyterian Church, Omagh.

There is a very beautiful minor hall in Trinity which is called "The Wee Johnny Room"

There is a brass plaque on the wall with the words "The chairs in this room were provided by the members of "The Wee Johnny Club" October 1957.

These chairs were very nice indeed They were light oak and red leather seats. They are still as good as new. The final address was given in 1958 as a official thank you to the Wee Johnny Club.

Parcel from Wee Johnny

Boys and girls on Friday morning I received a mysterious parcel from the postman. It was a registered parcel, which told me it contained something valuable. It wasn't very big, but it was heavy for its size, and it took 2/6 to send it through the post. When I got it I wondered what was in it and who had sent it. The postmark told me it was posted in Omagh, and when I shook it I could hear something rattling inside. What do you think was in it? I'm sure you would never guess. It was a box with 400 silver 3d. pieces. But what was it for, and who was it from? It was a present to help with the building of the Church Hall and it was from Wee Johnny. Isn't that wonderful! £5 from wee Johnny, all in 3d. pieces, and with the parcel was a letter.

Among other things this is what it said - "Young though I may be, I have, nevertheless, been watching with much interest the activities of Trinity Church and it has occurred to me that all these improvements and extensions which you and your co-workers have undertaken are for the benefit of every wee Johnny and wee Mary who are members of our Church Sunday School, and I feel we have a lot to be thankful for.

An idea struck me that it would be a great thing if I could gather up 3d. bits until I'd have £5, and then present it to you for the Building Fund. Of course I had to give up some of my usual treats, like the packet of Spangles and the weekly comic - but strangely enough they did not seem so very important when I set my heart on reaching this other goal.

I am sending my 400 3d. bits with this letter and already I feel I have just bought a £5 share in something very worthwhile. How would it do if all the children did the same?"

Isn't that a lovely letter and isn't it a great idea? I'm sure there are lots of boys and girls in Trinity who would like to have a share with wee Johnny in the building of the Hall Extension. I have been thinking a lot about it since I got that letter, and I hope in a week or two to start a scheme by which all the boys and girls can help. As you understand it will take a little time to work all the details, but, in the meantime, you could start to collect 3d. bits. And it would be a great thing, if through the inspiration and example of wee Johnny, the boys and girls of Trinity could contribute, say a hundred pounds in 1957, to the Hall Extension Fund.

Announcing the Wee Johnny Club

You remember last Sunday I told you about the box of 3d pieces I had received from Wee Johnny, and the suggestion in his letter that other boys and girls in the congregation might like to help with the new Hall by saving 3d. bits. Well this week I noticed another parcel, not from wee Johnny, but from a lady. It was too big a parcel to send through the post, so you can guess it wasn't a parcel of 3d. pieces. It was a parcel with ten big beautiful boxes of chocolates, and I haven't eaten one of them yet. You know why? Because they are not for me, they are for you, yes for you! They are for the first 10 boys or girls who save one Pound in 1957 and present it to the Building Fund. And this is how we're going to do it. We are going to start a Wee Johnny Club. All who join it will get a badge and a box to hold 20 3d. bits. When it is full they hand it in and get another box, and we will keep it going all through 1957. I have ordered boxes from Belfast and have written to England for special badges and when they arrive all who wish can join the club. But there is one rule we will all have to keep very strictly. It is this. All the money given must be money saved or earned by the boys and girls themselves. The purpose of the Club is not to collect money from others, but to encourage us to give something of our own. It would be a great thing if some part of the New Extension, or some of its furniture could be presented as a gift from the boys and girls. Anyone who wants to help in this effort can begin now by putting aside any spare 3d. pieces and by planning what they can do to earn something for the Fund.

Wee Johnny Club - Boxes & Cards

Boys and girls I told you last Sunday that if you wanted to join the Wee Johnny Club you could get your Membership Cards and your Boxes today. This is one of the Boxes . . . . It is inscribed on the top "The Wee Johnny Club, Trinity Church Omagh"; on the bottom of it there is a number, just to make sure that your box doesn't get mixed up with anyone else's. There is a little slit on the top to let you put in 3d pieces, and the Box holds about 5/= of big 3d pieces.

This is one of the membership cards . . . . It is printed on the front just like the top of the Box, only there is also a space for your name. Let me read you what it says inside . . . . Then there is a space to record the amount you have given.

I am sorry the badges haven't arrived yet. But they are being made specially in England, and as soon as they come every member of the Club will get one to wear.

Then there's something else you are going to get when you join the Club. You would never guess what it is. You are going to get two new Uncles. Uncle John and Uncle Herbie - Mr. John Cathcart and Mr. Herbert Todd, who are going to give out the Cards and Boxes and keep a record of all your contributions. The young people who go out to the Primary Sunday School will get their Cards and Boxes during the Sunday School today. The older children will get theirs in Church after the service this morning. Each member will only get one Box at a time. When that is full, bring it to Church, any Sunday and hand it in to Uncle John and Uncle Herbie after the service. And remember I still have those ten big boxes of chocolates for the first 10 who contribute £1.

Now I hope all the boys and girls and all their Mammies and Daddies will remember the rule of the Club . . . I can visualise that the Mammies of Trinity are going to have few dishes to wash in 1957, and the Daddies few shoes to clean or fires to set. But I hope whatever little job the members of the Club are asked to do that they will do it willingly and well. Remember always, that this is your form of service to the Kingdom of God. And whatever you do, do it heartily, as unto the Lord.

Wee Johnny Club

Instead of a story I want to say a few words to the boys and girls about the Wee Johnny Club. How many members do you think are in the Club? There are 87. All of them have boxes for the money they earn or save and which they want to give to the Hall Extension Fund. Some of those 87 members have already got their second box and some have even got their third. Nearly all the 10 boxes of chocolates have already been won, but nobody need be disappointed about that because at the end of the year we are going to give a prize to all the boys and girls who have returned their boxes. Nor need any of you be disappointed if somebody else has already given more than you. Remember you have a whole year, until the end of 1957, and perhaps those who keep at it steadily will have given more by the end of the year than those who start off with a great burst of enthusiasm. And how much do you think we have saved already? I'm not going to tell you that, because I want you to find out for yourselves. How many of you have noticed the Wee Johnny Club barometer? If you haven't noticed it, you can see it in the porch when you are leaving the Church today. The barometer was made by Uncle John, and its purpose is to show how much has been returned every month. If you look at it you will see that in January the total was £6 and that of course includes Wee Johnny's own 400 3ds. I can tell you there will be a big change on it next Sunday, because the total for February will be shown and I know you will all be surprised when you see how much it is. So keep your eyes open next Sunday when you are coming into Church.

There's just one other thing I want to mention. Can you guess what it is? The Wee Johnny Club badges. I told you we had to get them made in England and it has taken longer than we thought, but I am glad to say, you are going to get them today. This is one of the badges. Round the outside it says - The Wee Johnny Club, Trinity Church, Omagh and in the centre there is a picture of Wee Johnny himself. All the members of the Club are asked to wait at the close of the service today to get their badges. When you get them I hope you will all wear them, especially on Sunday. I hope you will always be proud to be a member of the Wee Johnny Club, and if anyone asks you what the Club is for, tell them what is printed on your membership card. 'The object of the Club is to encourage the boys and girls to help with the extension to the Church Hall in 1957'.

The Wee Johnny Club - Thanksgiving Service

Boys and girls, the service today is a special service to give thanks to God for the completion of the work at the Church Hall and I am very glad that you have had a share in this work. Since the beginning of the year the members of the Wee Johnny Club have been saving their 3d. pieces and already they have given over £100. If you work that out you will find that it is more than 8,000 3d. pieces. When the Club started some people thought if we raised £50 during the year we would be doing very well, and so we would. But the total has risen so steadily that we decided to buy beautiful chairs for one of the rooms in the new building. And if we keep on saving until the end of the year we will have enough money to pay for them all. You will be glad to know that the chairs have already been used. Last Sunday, we had 4 Sunday School classes in the Wee Johnny room, and as well as that it was used for the Primary Sunday School - for the wee ones who go out during the service. And when we start our mid-week service in November the chairs will be used every Wednesday as well. So you see, your 3ds. have been used to buy something beautiful and something useful too. That shows you what God can do when we bring our gifts to Him. That's what He can do with your life and mine. He can make us beautiful, as Christ was beautiful, and He can make us useful as Christ was useful in the service of the Kingdom. There is no better way to show our gratitude and no way more pleasing to God, that just to give Him the love, service and devotion of our hearts and lives. Will you do that today?

Wee Johnny Club - Thank You

The message for the boys and girls can be summed up in two words. Can you guess what they are? There are two words which I hope you never forget. What are they? THANK YOU. A great big thank you, underlined. That is what I want to say to you today. But why? Well you remember, just this month last year, I told you about a parcel I had received from Wee Johnny with 400 3d pieces in it and the suggestion that we might try to get the boys and girls to help to build the new Hall Extension. That's how we started the Wee Johnny Club and all through the year you have been giving your boxes full of 3ds. I remember when the Club started, some of us thought that if the members raised £25 or £50 they would be doing well. But gradually the total rose month after month until it had passed all our hopes and expectations. Today I want to tell you the total for the year. You would never guess how much it is. LISTEN: £160-13-11. Isn't that wonderful? I think it's terrific and I want to thank you all very much. Before the Hall was opened in October we bought all the chairs in the Wee Johnny Room, and some chairs for the kitchen too, and we put up a plaque on the wall upstairs, and at that time we didn't know if we would be able to pay for it all. But there's no doubt about it now, with over £160. How many 3ds. do you think are in that? Over 12,800 and if they were put side by side they would stretch almost 300 yards, from here to the courthouse. Isn't that great? Altogether there were 96 members in the Club. One little girl gave over £20, all of which she saved or earned herself. That could put a whole lot of bigger people to shame. It just shows you what you can do when your heart is really in a thing. Another girl, much smaller, gave over £9 and 7 others, some of them in one family gave £4 each. Boys and girls, you have all done wonderfully well, from the tiniest tot up. And I want to thank you all most sincerely. I hope you will always be proud of the part you had in the building of the new extension and that your example will be an inspiration to others.

Then I want to say "Thank you" too to Uncle John and Uncle Herbie, who all year kept the records and marked your cards and organised the whole Club. We could never have done without them. And now there's just one other thing - Uncle John and Uncle Herbie are going to give you a party sometime soon. I will tell you about that later, but in the meantime on behalf of the whole congregation, to all the members of the Wee Johnny Club, I want to say THANK YOU very much.

Index